Two Jewish-born Families in the Adirondacks: A Series of Transgenerational Sketches

Lawrence M. Ginsburg

For Alice C. Waugh of Lincoln, Massachusetts, my composition guru and reliable co-pilot whose "soft landing" glides homeward I've tried to emulate.

ISBN 978-1-66788-857-6

Library of Congress Control Number: 2022923013

Cover images (property of the author): The former trail sign near Ausable Club pointing toward base of Mt. Noonmark (top), and the marker on tree atop summit of Mt. Marshall, more than 4,360 feet above sea level. See the U.S. Geological Survey topographical map at coordinates 44° 07' 30" N and 74° 00' 30" W (bottom).

Contents

Only the mountain has lived long enough to listen objectively to the howl of the wolf.
　— Aldo Leopold, *A Sand Country Almanac and Sketches Here and There* (1949, p. 129)

Some mountains are content in their singularity,
or long for further mountains,
or maybe don't even notice that they are mountains.
　— Jason Wheeler, *Shelley Orgel* (2019, p. 15)

In such a way do my mountains long for foothills.
　— Julian Barnes, *Flaubert's Parrot* (1984, p. 150)

Preface

Felix Adler (1851-1933) and Louis Marshall (1856-1929) were born on opposite sides of the Atlantic Ocean. Their lives spanned eras in Jewish history reaching from the mid-19th century through the first third of the 20th century. Both ultimately settled in New York City and generally did not characterize one another in adversarial tones—at least publicly—on the printed page.

The author's thumbnail vignettes[1] about these two men, their spouses and extended family members are brief in scope. The orbits each multigenerational clan converged upon several occasions. Further characteristics of the undulating terrain[2] of upstate New York seem worth mentioning in gauging related socioeconomic conditions.

---

[1] Although he is neither a professional genealogist nor an archival fact-checker, he researched records at the Keene Valley Historical Society in Keene Valley, N.Y., where a transcript of Felix Adler's widow Helen Adler's address of Sept. 9, 1939 is archived. He has referenced other such institutional repositories in Ithaca and New York, N.Y.; Cincinnati, Ohio; and Berkeley, Calif. He has also credited data from sources including the two-volume *Autobiography of Andrew D. White* (1905), publications authored by M. M. Silver (2013) and the two-volume compendium compiled by editor Charles Reznikoff (1957) entitled *Louis Marshall: Champion of Liberty*. Other sources that were temporarily inaccessible due to the Covid-19 pandemic lockdowns are items in the "Felix Adler Papers" [MS#0011] collections at the Butler Library of Columbia University, as well as other items concerning the William Channing Russel collections at the Kroch Library of Cornell University.

[2] For contextual purposes about upstate New York geography, the Laurentian range includes the Adirondack Mountains while the Allegheny range includes the geologically older Catskill Mountains. To the west are the glacially formed Finger Lakes. Imagine pressing your right hand on a regional map with fingers stretching southward to the equator. Of the remaining "fingers," generally stretching in a north-to-south axis, one would simulate Cayuga Lake. Indigenous to this area was the Iroquois Confederacy. The Native American tribes were led by legendary Chief Hiawatha (also known as "The Great Peacemaker"). He headed its long house near present-day Syracuse, N.Y.

1. Felix Adler's Youth and Early Adult Life

Rabbi Samuel L. Adler (1809-1891) and his wife Henrietta (née Frankfurter) Adler were born in former duchies collectively known as the *Germanisch Konfederarasi.* Such realms were to become modern Germany. They arrived in New York City in 1857 with sons Isaac and Felix Adler. Their American-born sister Sarah[1] joined the family the following year.

Rabbi Adler led a Jewish Sabbath service following the death of Pres. Abraham Lincoln on Apr. 15, 1865 in Manhattan's Temple Emanu-El. According to one account:

"The entire Congregation stood and recited the Kaddish [the Jewish prayer for the dead]…Rabbi Adler was so overcome with grief he could not speak…though a few weeks later he likened Lincoln to Moses, both emancipators of slaves…" (Rock, p. 19).

Rabbi Alan W. Miller opined about the reputed Civil War perspectives of Rabbi S. L. Adler and by extension, his 14-year-old son Felix, as follows: "[T]here is a curious paradox between the fact that his father [Rabbi S. L. Adler], wedded though he was to the Abolitionist cause, never once raised the moral issue of slavery from the pulpit out of fear of his middle-class Jewish congregation's economic proclivities…" (p. 380).[2] After a 12-paragraph detour, further commentary about the remainder of Rabbi Miller's excerpted argument pertaining to Felix resumes.

Felix was almost 15 years old when a headline in the New York Times heralded that, for the first time in recorded history, an Englishman had stood upon the summit of the Matterhorn in the European Alps. According to the later recollections of Helen Adler (née Goldman), his future wife, "he craved the joy of mountain-climbing during his student years abroad. In the Tyrol and Switzerland, he had ascended some of the most difficult and dangerous peaks…" (H. Adler, p. 2).

A higher education abroad was becoming *de rigueur* for male descendants of both sides of Rabbi Adler's European-born families. Several had distinguished themselves as renowned Talmudic scholars. After graduating from Columbia College,[3] Felix returned to Germany for immersion in a regimen of Jewish studies. Subsequently, Heidelberg University awarded him a doctorate with the highest honors. Kraut (1979) noted that "Felix's success in Arabic was especially gratifying to Samuel, for his son's mastery of an 'important adjunct to Jewish theology, renewed his hope that Felix would succeed him at [Temple] Emanu-El in New York City'" (ibid., p. 49). Kraut added:

> "On Saturday, Oct. 11, 1873, on the Festival of Sukot [sic], Felix Adler delivered his first and only sermon at Temple Emanu-El, entitled 'The Judaism of the Future.' The temple was crowded. There, of course, was much anxiety to hear him [Felix] in his father's pulpit—as an American Rabbi is somewhat of a novelty. Few people, however, could have anticipated his address, for his Temple Sermon essentially propounded a new religion which he had devised in Germany. While he identified this religion as 'the Judaism of the future,' the sermon's new religious orientation and innovative homiletical format surprised the audience" (ibid., p. 76).

To the father's embarrassment and disappointment, the trustees of Temple Emanu-El deemed that Felix was unwelcome to preach from their pulpit. He was forced to refocus his energies elsewhere.

Ezra Cornell (1807-1874),[4] as a co-founder of the university that bears his name, treasured a motto: "I would found an institution where any person can find instruction in any study!" Toward the end of his life, the remarkable "any person" clause proved problematic for an array of legislators attending the 97th session of the New York State Senate.[5] By then, both he and his co-founder Andrew Dickson White (1832-1918) were ex-Senators. A published transcript of the latter's testimony (White, 1873b) before the same body illustrates how he distanced himself from any appearance of personal antisemitic and/or pro-Christian zealotry: "We have several Jewish students in our institution, and among them some of our very best students, and I would never sanction anything that would infringe on their privileges, deprive them of their rights or to degrade them in any manner" (ibid., p. 248).

Cornell University co-founder and future Pres. White was born in Homer, N.Y., in Cortland County midway between Ithaca and Syracuse. The respective adult lives of both Cornell and White unfurled within a geographical range of less than 50 miles. The pre-adolescent home of Ezra Cornell was situated within a settlement known as the Quaker Basin a mile easterly from the village of DeRuyter in Madison County, which borders both Onondaga and Cortland Counties (the latter of which adjoined Tompkins County, where his adult home was situated). Inaugural Pres. White credited himself with having recruited Englishman Goldwin Smith, the Regius Professor of History at Oxford, to become their newborn institution's crown jewel. He had achieved international eminence as an anti-Disraeli historian. A snobbish condescension of Jews unerringly infused his academic *œuvre* (Mendelson, 2008, pp. 49 and 53-54).

Highlighting the early development of Cornell University, Prof. William Channing Russel (1814-1896) was elected to the chair of modern languages and adjunct professor of history at Cornell University on Feb. 13, 1867. By mid-1870 he was its first Vice President and Acting President on June 14, 1876. At the end of the spring semester, his tenure as such was not renewed. (Keller, 1961, p. 1).

From the banks of the Neckar River where Felix had previously meandered along Heidelberg's Philosopher's Walk *(Philosophenweg)* to Ithaca's gorges in upstate New York, the distance—apart from a hiatus in Manhattan—is approximately 4,000 miles. In 1874, after the banker Joseph Seligman had attended a few of Felix's public lectures, negotiations were undertaken to fund "a visiting professorship in Hebrew and Oriental Literature" for him at Cornell University, which included a stipend for a three-month teaching tenure plus an apartment on University grounds" while residing in Ithaca *(ibid.,* p. 95). In letters to his younger sister Sarah, he extolled the rugged beauty of the campus *(ibid.,* pp. 98 & 244, fn. 93).

Certain communications about the Seligman/White negotiations survive. Included is a letter from White to an unspecified correspondent (see "Felix Adler Papers MS #0011") who—judging from its contents—was likely Seligman. It was penned on Mar. 10, 1874, reputedly after a "meeting of the Executive Committee of our Board of Directors brought up the matter of a professorship or lecture such as would meet the ideas of Dr. Adler" (White, 1873a, p. 1). Pres. White suggested the creation of a $100,000 endowment fund generating interest to create an appropriate post for Prof. Adler *(ibid.,* p. 3). At some point, a Seligman/White meeting presumably took place in New York City at which Seligman obligated himself to escrow a capital fund of $20,000 whose income accrued in favor of Cornell University. With a guaranteed annual income of 7%, such a fund would generate $4,200 toward Felix's salary over a period of three years (Whalen, 2003, pp. 12-14).

Pursuant to the aforementioned understanding, an April 9, 1874 letter from Pres. White to Seligman cemented Felix's engagement to serve as an active-duty faculty member at Cornell from 1874-1877; his salary as a professor "is fixed at Fourteen Hundred Dollars per annum whenever received from the respected donors" with the annual duration of his employment "not less than one trimester of twelve weeks" (see Felix Adler Paper MS #0011).

During April of 1874, by the reckoning of then-Cornell University Vice Pres. Russel, Prof. Adler "had commenced his series of lectures to large numbers of attentive listeners from both the University and the town." According to Russel (as reported by Keller, *ibid.*), Prof. Adler "spoke with eloquence in expressing his desire to cultivate religion at Cornell and in appealing to the students to co-operate with him in his effort. Russel, not realizing that religion, as apart from religions, was in Adler's plan, looked forward to the great liberal thinking and educational effect such a concept would have on those who had never before been subjected to such an idea. Two months later, however, Russel was reporting much 'hissing and sissing and rushing a steam and bursting of bubbles in the teapot' as concerned Adler (Keller, p. 22). As reported in Russel's further commentaries:

> "On one occasion the new professor [Adler] had described the immaculate conception of Buddha and given as the reason for people adhering to such a mistaken idea the believers' conviction that the natural act was itself evil. On another occasion, Adler had stated that the idea of a God was not general with the race but arrived with the development of civilization. While Russel was not personally shaken by Adler's contradictions of orthodox and evangelical beliefs, he was extremely anxious that Adler's excellent message not be compromised or destroyed by unthinking remarks like those referring to Buddha's calling on all those who were 'weary and heavy laden' and his coming to be a 'Savior of them.' Such, Russel held, were unnecessary and more than likely to call down the wrath of the 'righteous.' Russel admired Adler's ability but regretted his tendency to 'talk down' to people, who he, Russel felt, no doubt, regarded as his inferiors. Moreover, it was Russel's impression that Adler mistook opposition for progress and the number of his opponents for the measure of his own gains" *(ibid.,* pp. 22-23).

Pres. White ultimately came to assert that Adler left Cornell of his own accord. Such pretensions seem historically absurd; it was disingenuous for him to have ever claimed otherwise. Rather than addressing concerns of his institution's Board of Trustees concerning the continuation of Adler's split-term appointment, he asserted that members of Cornell University's governing board reputedly "prefer an incumbent who can reside steadily at the University and who can give his whole attention to it" (Kraut, p. 104). Instances of nonresident faculty domiciled principally in Toronto (Goldwin Smith), Boston (Louis Agassiz), Providence (George William Curtis) and elsewhere had not beforehand been deemed aberrant. The most flagrant abuse of such an academic hierarchy at Cornell University was embodied in nominally absent Pres. White's own two-year hiatus as an overseas domiciliary while serving as ambassador to Germany. [6]

One of Dr. Adler's acolytes treasured a "remembrance of having been a participant" in his *Union for Higher Life,* as he explained in his book *All in a Lifetime* (Morgenthau). According to his first-hand account, "every man expected purity from his wife, it was his duty to enter the marriage state in the same condition" *(ibid.,* pp. 94-97). By the reckoning of historian Kraut, the union originated with "a very small group of selected people initiated at Cornell and devoted to moral purity, celibacy in bachelorhood, and simplicity in dress and manners" (Kraut, p. 47). Members had initially aspired to "starting a co-operative community for ourselves..." (Morgenthau p. 97). The intent of their goals was to strive toward implementing an idealistic social credo.[7] According to the rationale of Dr. Adler, as quoted by Morgenthau:

> "American Jews could adjust themselves to the land in which they were living and drop all that they had had to adhere to in Ghettoized Europe. He [Felix] was filled with an enthusiastic desire to remedy the glaring evils, not only of the Jews, but of the entire community: he could diagnose our ills and prescribe a remedy" *(ibid.)*

For Felix, Jews were neither ordained to forsake Biblical identities nor destined to simulate Old World cultures or merely distinguish themselves via social concerns and good deeds. His moral idealism, for others, may have seemed imperious. Conjecturally, he may simply have felt a need to protect the expansive philosophical tenets he had been espousing in behalf of his Society for Ethical Culture against emerging rival movements.

Missing from the concluding language of Rabbi Miller's assertion (see third paragraph of this chapter) is this afterthought: "Whilst the son went out of his way, at Cornell for example, *pour épater le bourgeois,* historians should at least give a nod in the direction of the unconscious these days" (Miller, p. 380). Consistent with Rabbi Miller's speculations, it is undisputable that Felix, in Rabbi Miller's view, harbored conflicting thoughts— both conscious and unconscious—throughout life about his adult family's stance during the Civil War. Vestiges of personal shame about their silence during our nation's biggest bloodbath seemed to haunt him. The juxtaposition of his father's belated eulogy after Pres. Lincoln's assassination and Pres. White's choice not to extend the junior Adler's employment at Cornell University is spurious. For some readers, the "curious paradox" cited in the third paragraph stems from an attempt to link a father's retrospective "sins" with his son's arguably heretic "isms" and/or doctrines. It seems obvious that Rabbi Miller attempted to conflate two historical events (the Civil War and the birth of Cornell University) that in fact had been separated by more than a decade.

During the era that Felix was a resident academician in Ithaca, manifestations of America's Christianity were omnipresent. Yet, according to Cornell University records ("Statistics of the Class of 1874" in Cornell University Archives #41-4-554), 40 of the 72 members of the graduating class during the first year of Felix's employment (69 men and three women) identified themselves as adherents of specific Gentile sects and one as a Buddhist. A plurality of the remaining 32 graduates characterized their religious persuasions as independent, pagan, liberal, rationalist, neutral, free, of no sect, undecided or the nonsectarian Society of Friends.[8] Rants such as those that Goldwin Smith often voiced about the threats of disguised "Judaizers" to western civilizations were resminiscent of "not very subtle forms of antisemitism and racism. In *The Revival of Antisemitism* (1921), Felix Adler declared: "Goldwin Smith in conversation once expressed his misgivings, lest in case of strain, the clan feelings of the Jews might overcome their patriotic feelings" (F. Adler, 1921, p. 9).

It stretches one's imagination to reckon that, even in the loose so-called WASP-ish vernacular of the era in which they lived, Pres. White had been ignorant of Goldwin Smith's incendiary prejudices.

Felix Adler described his sojourns in what was popularly still know as "the land of Dixie," opining about post-slavery trauma characterizing Negro life during the Reconstructionist Jim Crow period. He patronizingly described the traditions of *noblesse oblige,* the crudeness of democracy, the failed Freedmen's Bureau, a New vs. Old South, and the obvious disparity in levels of black and white socioeconomic opportunities as well as his own aversion to doctrinaire socialism.

Late in life, Felix was quoted as having voiced his opinion that for those teaching history, "the liberation of the slaves should be treated as the starting point for the social mission of the American Republic" (Friess, 1944, p. 5).[9] No longer was it feasible for Felix to deny the reality of a grave site where the abolitionist "John Brown's body lay a-moldering" in North Elba, N.Y. His corpse is still interred less than a 10-mile hike across Cascade Mountain from Felix's former sylvan "paradise" in St. Huberts, N.Y. In contrast to Ralph Waldo Emerson's adulation of John Brown— likening him to the quintessential American "Saint" of the anti-slavery movement—Felix may have simply maintained a "middle of the road" philosophical stance. Instead, he may have ruminated about whether John Brown had been a murderer, a traitor or a madman? Or, perchance an oscillating funerary mirage?[9]

Although their matriculations as Cornell University undergraduates did not overlap, acclaimed naturalist/educators John Henry Comstock (1849-1931) and Anna Botsford Comstock (1854-1930) were married in Ithaca on Oct. 7, 1878. Prof. Felix Adler initially met his aforesaid (then single) male student during the latter's senior year in 1873. Comstock's future wife matriculated the semester following his graduation while he continued as a fledgling instructor and enthusiastic disciple of the younger Prof. Adler. She ultimately graduated with the Class of 1885. Mrs. Comstock had earlier composed a vignette about their respective first-hand interrelationships with Prof. Adler. An abbreviated quotation from an edition of her autobiography, posthumously published in 1952, ensues:

> "Felix Adler... was young, attractive, and brilliant, and was regarded as a radical, although his views would seem conservative now. He was dreaming of a future of helpfulness to mankind and this dream he has lived to see realized in his great ethical movement. His classroom was thronged with enthusiastic young men who thought for themselves and enjoyed the daring leadership of 'The Young Eagle,' as they affectionately called him. A Sunday afternoon class, organized for social betterment, met in Professor Russel's study at his home on Seneca Street" (Comstock, p. 48).

Elsewhere, discussion has centered on changing the dedication of a 100-year-old building named after Goldwin Smith. Alternatively, it has been suggested that "a plaque be installed which explains that his writings reveal 'a stridently anti-Semitic reading of European history'" (Altschuler and Kramnick, p. 38; Davis, p. 1; Giaforte and Greene, p. 1). A growing number of institutions have recently begun to re-evaluate the time-tarnished statuary gracing their quadrangles eulogizing notable benefactors.

---

[1] Younger sister Sarah (née Adler) Goldman married Julius Goldman. The couple—in keeping with old-fashioned Jewish traditions—named one of their daughters Hetty Goldman (1882-1972) in honor of their newborn's predeceased maternal grandmother Henrietta. This marital merger ripened to create a further retinue of Sachs descendents summering at St. Huberts.

[2] It seems implausible for Rabbi S.L. Adler, as a pre-Civil War immigrant, to have empathized with the political agenda of the Know-Nothing Party. In a lecture he gave on Apr. 25, 1886 at Chickering Hall in New York City entitled "Reforms Needed in the Pulpit," Felix faulted "the American Church in the late anti-slavery struggle…with noble and honorable exceptions but…as a whole, either remained timidly neutral, or was arrayed on the side of the oppressor rather than the oppressed; that a very large number of the clergy, while that struggle was going on, were busy heaping up quoting quotation from the Bible mountain high as a barrier in the way of emancipation" (F. Adler, p. 4). Whether or not Felix had ever been ordained as a Jewish rabbi during his European sojourn in Berlin is unclear.

[3] At Columbia College, where brothers Isaac and Felix Adler matriculated in the Classes of 1868 and 1870, it has long been asserted that both "complained about Saturday exams" (McCaughey, p. 257).

[4] He reputedly had been banished from a local religious Society of Friends for his marriage to a non-Quaker wife.

[5] From its inception in 1865, Cornell University lay mired in the center of religious controversy as it became "one of the first universities founded as a nonsectarian institution and supported by state funds" (Kraut, p. 99).

[6] See Appendix II (infra, pp. 66-67).

[7] Joseph Seligman was elected President; the initial membership reputedly included "between three hundred and four hundred of the most prominent Jews of New York" (Olan, p. 6).

[8] Slighted by many Cornell University historians is an 1874 survey of undergraduate religiosities.

[9] Morgenthau's diary has this entry for Apr. 24, 1892: "We debated the simplicity of dress and the follies of extravagance. Then, as Dr. Adler wanted us to feel that we were doing something altruistic, the members of the Union jointly adopted eight children; some of them were half-orphans, and some had parents who could not support them properly; we employed a matron and hired a flat for her…" (Morgenthau, p. 97). Coincidentally, the colony of "perfectionists," known as the Oneida Community, had thrived near the geographic center of New York state. Excavated at Palmyra, N.Y. were the revered Scriptures of the Church of Latter-Day Saints. By 1890, William R. George began a "colorblind" summer refuge at a rural farm in Dryden, N.Y., that welcomed New York "ghetto-born lads and

girls whose basic heritage still seemed Jewish-oriented" (Ginsburg, 2010, p. 39). Neither the nominal Fresh Air youth movement nor the so-called Borscht Belt had yet coalesced as rural escape venues in the still-remote Catskill Mountains. After the George Junior Republic was incorporated in Freeville, N.Y., Syracuse Rabbi Adolph Gutmann, accompanied by a German-writing educator-administrator while he was traveling in North America, visited in 1895-1896 *(ibid.,* pp. 28-29 & 38).

2. Louis Marshall's Boyhood through Mid-life

Syracuse had been the virtual center of Marshall's universe throughout the first half of his life. The lives of his parents had inauspicious beginnings abroad. Bavarian-born Jacob Marshall (1830-1912) crossed the Atlantic Ocean in 1849 on a sailing vessel at age 19.[1] In 1853, sisters Zilli Strauss and Regina Strauss, together with a brother, emigrated from Württemberg in Germany to their "New World." Their harrowing journey to Halifax [in Canada] took 63 days; "the ship was brought into that port by mutineers after going through indescribable experiences" (Handlin, pp. ix-xli).[2] Two years later, the survivors ultimately settled in Syracuse, where Zilli married Jacob Marshall and Regina married David Stolz.

Unlike most marriages of the period, Jacob was younger than Zilli (ca. 1826-1910). She and her sister found employment as domestic servants. Jacob had emigrated "with only five francs (amounting to 95 cents in American money) in his pocket" (Rudolph, p. 16). He initially found work on railroads and Erie Canal construction gangs in upstate New York. Thereafter, "he began as a pack-peddler, did not do too well and opened a fruit stand" in Syracuse *(ibid.,* pp. 16-17).

The elder Marshall eventually established himself as a processor of raw hides and skins. Native American trappers from the Iroquois confederacy of tribes populating the region's nearby hunting grounds were among his suppliers. With a horse and wagon, he was able to ascend the foothills leading from Syracuse southeast toward the Catskill Mountains[3] as well as northeast toward the Adirondack Mountains. Curing the eviscerated animal pelts required barrels of salt blocks that were harvested as a byproduct of evaporated brine. Unlimited quantities gushed from springs alongside the shores of nearby Onondaga Lake, a glacially formed hypersaline body of water. Louis, his family's first-born, later reminisced about the "hard manual labor which is now prohibited under the Child Labor Laws" (see Appendix III) that he had endured as a juvenile.

As a boy, Louis was unquestionably familiar with the semi-historical Hiawatha ("The Great Peacemaker"),[3] who was the Onondaga chief and leader of the Iroquois Confederacy. His intertribal longhouse had been situated near Syracuse since before the Revolutionary War in the Finger Lakes area of upstate New York. By way of Longfellow's poetic license, Hiawatha's legend was repositioned from the shores of Onondaga Lake to the wilderness frontiers of Minnesota, where the hero supposedly fell in love with Minnehaha.

During the Civil War, Syracuse was notorious as a hotbed of abolitionist sympathizers. Part A of *Israelites in Blue and Gray: Unchronicled Tales from Two Cities* is a tribute to Company A of the Union Army's 149th Volunteer Infantry Regiment (Ginsburg, 2001). This unit was mainly raised, recruited, funded, uniformed and led by officers from Syracuse's Jewish community. Its battle flag, sewn by the "Jewish Ladies of Syracuse" (p. 8), was severely tattered by Confederate bullets and artillery. Marshall was a boy of eight when Pres. Lincoln was assassinated.

Syracuse historian Rudolph in *From a Minyan to a Community: A History of the Jews of Syracuse* stated:
> "Debating clubs were in vogue. In 1868, as a precocious youngster of twelve, he [Marshall] joined one of these clubs [then meeting next door to his boyhood home in the basement of Temple Society of Concord] and was considered a leading debater... People wondered at his thorough knowledge of early American history, and in debates he would always be the passionate defender of the Constitution" (p. 103).

The Marshall youngster—unlike his father's abbreviated pack-peddler lot in life—was spared the fate of an immigrant adolescent such as W. Lee Provol, also known as Willie Provolsky, author of *The Pack Peddler* (subtitled "The Son of One of Them"). His autobiographical saga, centered in upstate Central New York, mirrored the poignant plights of less fortunate families who had to scratch out a livelihood as "greenhorn" entrepreneurs. Willie—unlike the the offspring of the Adler/Goldmark and Marshall/Lowenstein families born in the mid-19th century—set out for a week of travel away from home with "a stock of sundries" prepackaged at Thalheimer's, a regional wholesaler, that included an assorted inventory of fancy stationery, imported Swedish parlor matches, current newspapers, etc. According to the adult Willie's account, some of his fellow entrepreneurs acquired crucifixes, scapulars, rosaries, prayer books, medals, religious statues, etc. (pp. 46-47) for resale by swapping selected goods with rival Gentile peddlers. Unlike the juvenile Felix and Louis, Yiddish rather than German was the first language of both Provolskys.

Biographer M. M. Silver, in *Louis Marshall and the Rise of Jewish Ethnicity in America*, noted that "through 1876, [Marshall] belonged in Syracuse to the Andrew White Debating Society and contributed to publications issued by it" (p. 543, fn. 29).

Marshall[4] had long resided near in an area east of Salina Street that was vernacularly known as "Jewtown." Nearby was a major metropolitan bridge spanning the Erie Canal in metropolitan Syracuse. Mansions belonging to banker-members of the extended White families were situated along James Street, a thoroughfare named after William James (1771-1832).[5] It stretched eastward along the northerly/newer side of the Erie Canal.

Future educator White and Louis Marshall were nearly a quarter-century apart in age. The senior eminence had served for a term as Louis Marshall's New York state senator. He funded *The Monthly Debater,*[6] a publication staffed by Syracuse High School students. He had also been a co-founder of the Onondaga Club—an association for literary and recreational purposes—in Syracuse. The extended White clan were active participants in the anti-slavery movement represented by such men as Gerrit Smith, Wendell Phillips, William Lloyd Garrison, John Park Hale, Samuel Joseph May and Frederick Douglass.

Following Marshall's graduation from Syracuse High School in 1874, he served as an office boy/clerk in the local office of Nathaniel B. Smith and caught the attention of William C. Ruger, who was later elected Chief Judge of the New York State Court of Appeals. During the 1876-77 academic year, Louis attended what then was known as the Law School at Columbia College in New York City. There, according to biographer Silver, he was recognized by Prof. Theodore William Dwight and faculty colleagues (see also Ogden, 1959) as an outstanding legal scholar. Enrollment over a two-year period was at that time required to qualify for an academic degree, and the Marshall family was unable to afford subsidizing further study in New York City beyond his abbreviated matriculation.

In Marshall's June 15, 1897 correspondence, he alluded to his circumscribed formal legal training. One biographer observed:
"Later in life, Marshall remarked sparingly about his law school year; but fragments he left corroborate a common-sense supposition of the significant impression it made upon him. Forty years [afterwards]…he corresponded with Ansel Judd Northrup, a County Judge from Onondaga County, who dabbled as a writer about nature and political issues. At the start of Marshall's studies, a member of the bar in Syracuse invited him to his house,

where he introduced the young prodigy to Dwight. In 1917, Marshall recalled this meeting 'as one of the brightest moments in my life' that 'marked the beginning of a most pleasant and inspiring relationship with our great teacher.' Were he 'to attain a century of years,' Marshall would never forget the evening" (Silver, pp. 11-12 and 547, fn. 39; see Appendix III for further autobiographical commentary)

Marshall was admitted to the New York state bar on Jan. 8, 1874 and became a junior partner in the Syracuse firm of Ruger, Jenney, Brooks, French & Marshall. After senior partner Ruger's election to head the highest court in the Empire State, James B. Brooks left the renamed firm in 1895 to become dean of the Syracuse University College of Law.[7] Porter M. French then exited the partnership to practice law in Rochester, leaving Edwin S. Jenney and Marshall.

A Rochester-based weekly newspaper, *The Jewish Tidings* ("A Fearless Exponent of Progressive Judaism!") began publication in upstate New York's three principal cities (Buffalo, Rochester and Syracuse) on Feb. 5, 1887. Three Syracuse subscribers—including Marshall and a couple of his physician friends—voiced positive opinions in the May 2, 1890 issue about "the proposition of supplementary religious purposes of supplementary religious purposes and/or lectures contemplating regular Sunday attendance beyond more traditional available options" (Ginsburg, 2010, pp. 11-12). The following week, a letter to the editor from the Syracuse Rabbi at Temple Society of Concord ("Rev. Dr. A. Guttman, Syracuse") stated: "I am opposed to divine services on Sunday for Jews, not to Sunday lectures." Further opponents of the referenced opinions of Marshall and his colleagues asserted that they were attempting to "stab the Jewish Sabbath in the back." Apart from such intramural debates, few sympathies were asserted for the local merchants who kept their stores open on Saturday for the patronage of Gentile customers.

A segment of the monograph subtitled "A Jewish Orphanage" explicated the role of Marshall (1908/1909, pp. 5-13) in founding such an institution in Rochester during the last decade of the 19th century. At a subsequent national conference about practices in Jewish-sponsored child care institutions including settlement houses, orphanages and reformatories,[8] Marshall *(ibid.)* called for "intensified religious instruction and observance including the teaching of Hebrew in such institutions," stating that it "must not be a Judaism that is apologetic... it must not be a Judaism in name only...it must not be a Judaism of the sterilized... variety only" (p. 12).

By the time Marshall relocated in New York City in 1894, Syracuse was no longer the center of his universe. Thereafter, his feisty prowess as a practicing constitutional lawyer manifested itself both nationally and internationally; the skilled rhetoric beneath the challenging stances he crafted is as authentic today as it was over a century ago.

In a posthumously published article, author J. W. Wise (1928), described Marshall as:

"the country boy[9] [who]...has never outgrown that background, has never, despite his many years of urban residence, become wholly citified...[yet]...played so many roles upon the Jewish scene that one might write about him at equal length as statesman, educator, religious revivalist, philanthropist" (pp. 181-182).

Another chronicler observed: "Mixed with this Americanism was a good portion of hometown loyalty. In later years, [Marshall] sometimes acted as though no one from Syracuse could do any wrong" (Rosenstock, p. 28).

Biographer Silver mused that "in April 1911, for the first time in his life, he [Marshall] celebrated the Passover Seder outside of Syracuse" (Silver, p. 209).

---

[1] By 1852, Jacob Marshall and David Stolz were boarding with the family of Gabriel Bondy (Bondy, p. 12). Then Zilli Straus married Jacob Marshall and her sister Regina Straus married David Stolz. The interrelationships were further compounded when the senior Marshall's sister Yetta married Jacob Stolz ("The Custom Boot and Shoe-Maker") in Syracuse. Both couples thereby became twice-consanguineous kindred *landsmen*. Parenthetically, it is noted that Marshall and prominent Chicago Rabbi Joseph Stolz—a son of the Stolz couple and cousin of Louis Marshall—collaborated with one another in nationally significant Jewish communal affairs continued throughout their respective lives.

[2] See the 43-page essay entitled "Introduction" In *Louis Marshall: Champion of Liberty,* C. Reznikoff, ed., vol. I. Philadelphia: The Jewish Publication Society of America (Handlin, pp. ix-xli).

[3] In the words of a recent biographer, Marshall's "environmental crusades are linked to his labors in the 1920s on behalf of African Americans and Native Americans" (Silver, p. 382).

[4] It may have come to the nearly 16-year-old Marshall's attention, as an avid reader of local Syracuse newspapers, that, during the month of October 1871, Pres.

White had been accused of having "descended to attend to the political affairs" of a statewide Republican Party convention in Syracuse while simultaneously representing his home district as a nonresident legislator and serving as Cornell University's first Pres.. In a lengthy letter attempting to exonerate White from the "the allegation that White had been deprived of part of his prestige and influence as a result of the politicking at Syracuse, Russel fairly scoffed and replied that the assaults and misrepresentations of partisan newspapers had only pointed up the Pres.'s exemplary citizenship and fair play" (Keller, p. 14). In 1898, a College of Forestry was created at Cornell University. It was defunded in 1903 over controversies involving the College's forestry practices in the Adirondacks. See also Chapter 15 for role of Louis Marshall in promoting such a successor institution in Syracuse, N.Y.

[5] James had arrived in Syracuse as a young Irish immigrant, became a local land speculator and subsequently relocated in Albany. There he fathered a brood that included a like-named son, William James, M.D., as well as author Henry James.

[6] The masthead in the Sept. 1876 issue (vol. I, no. 3) of *The Monthly Debater* published in Syracuse by members of the Andrew D. White Debating Society (a periodical "Devoted to Literature and Society and Melange") designated Louis Marshall as co-editor of its Literary Department. The listed cost for a single copy was 5¢. An available issue discloses that a couple of young adult chums from his Jewish neighborhood (Samuel R. Stern and Henry L. Elsner) were also active participants. One of the topics for discussion was related to the "wars with the Sioux which proceeds slowly, and every true American citizen awaits their extermination with impatience. Those who still adhere to the Quaker policy, ask that the Indians should be spared, but they forget the crimes perpetrated by these savages" (p. 1). It is likely that then-Pres. White and Marshall came face to face in the evening of Nov. 21, 1873. See also White (pp. 178-179, diary entry for June 2, 1869), Stern (pp. 24-32) and Silver (p. 543, fn. 9).

[7] The Syracuse University College of Law was launched in 1893, the same year in which Syracuse attorney Ernest Ingersoll White (1869-1957) graduated from Cornell University, where his uncle, Amb. White, had served as a co-founder. While Syracuse University was not launched until 1870, a program of law study at Cornell University had begun in 1887, some six years before E. I. White earned his baccalaureate degree in Ithaca. A succession of sites in the center of metropolitan Syracuse housed the fledgling institution. The last such edifice had been situated diagonally southwest of the Onondaga County Court House. In 1953, a new edifice on the university's main campus, was dedicated as the Ernest I. White College of Law some 60 years after its birth. Marshall would have known the philanthropist, who had been a native Syracuse attorney. Another replacement edifice, Dineen Hall, now serves as the home for the Syracuse University College of Law.

[8] See Marshall (1908/1909), "Proceedings of the 5th National Conference of

Jewish Charities" (pp. 112-122).

[9] Marshall also wrote: "I know something about practising in what is known as the country, because from 1878 to 1894, I practised in Syracuse…" (see Appendix III per 2/19/1929 letter at p. 1146 [LM/CR]) to "A Country Lawyer.")

3. Helen (née Goldmark) Adler (1859-1948)

Joseph J. Goldmark (1819-1881)—a physician, chemist and discoverer of red phosphorus—had been accused of high treason in Vienna. He fled the pre-1848 Habsburg Empire, settled in Brooklyn in 1850, and began to practice medicine while establishing himself as a prosperous American manufacturer of dynamite and percussion caps a decade before the start of the Civil War. The Goldmark & Conrad Factory near the Gowanus Canal in Brooklyn was producing munitions for the Northern war efforts when Pres. Lincoln was assassinated.

The year before the self-exiled Goldmark settled in America, his future in-laws, Gottlieb Wehle and Eleonore (née Fiegel) Wehle, emigrated with their extended family from Prague to the United States. Regina, their young daughter had early memories of crossing the Erie Canal westward in 1849 to the family's first home situated in the village of Madison[1] in Indiana halfway along the Ohio Valley between Louisville and Cincinnati before they eventually relocated in New York City. There, the senior Goldmark paterfamilias met and married Regina (née Wehle) Goldmark in 1856 where Helen, their eldest daughter, was born in 1859.

Unlike her academically prolific siblings (see Chapter 8), a paucity of publications flowed from Helen's pen.[2] In a widely read biography of her husband, there is only one instance in which she was mentioned in print (Kraut, p. 166).

Regina (née Wehle) Goldmark was widowed on Apr. 18, 1881. She was survived by a brood of seven daughters and one son. Her eldest daughter Helen Adler and Felix Adler were married during the previous year, and Helen was mobilized as a second matriarchal figure for her fatherless younger siblings. Among them was Josephine Clara Goldmark, then only 3½ years of age. During the summer season of 1881, the yet childless Adler couple chaperoned some of her half-orphaned sisters as co-borders with themselves in the Beede House at St. Huberts, N.Y. (Weston, pp.17-19). Early in 1883, the first of five children was born to the Adler couple.

––––––––––––––

[1] It was in Madison that Gottlieb Wehle became "president of the newly formed [Jewish] congregation in 1853" (Shevitz, 2007, p. 59). See Chapter 12 for references about the Brandeis clan.

[2] Over much of Helen's adult life, she appeared passively in favor of women's suffrage while opposed to unlimited public roles for women. The transcript of her lecture on Sept. 6, 1939 before the Keene Valley Historical Society entitled "Felix Adler, One of the Early Pioneers in Keene Valley at Beede's" is catalogued at the Keene Valley Archives in Keene Valley, N.Y. See also *Hints for the Scientific Observation and Study of Children* (H. Adler, 1891). Parenthetically, one of her younger sisters was to become the wife of Supreme Court Justice Louis D. Brandeis.

4. Florence (née Lowenstein) Marshall (1873-1916)

Florence's father Benedict Lowenstein (1831-1879) landed in New Orleans in 1854 and worked his way north along the Mississippi River to Memphis, where he and his brother founded a prosperous clothing company, B. Lowenstein & Bros. He met his wife Sophia (née Mendelson) Lowenstein (1845-1884), a native New Yorker, on a northern buying trip. Perhaps in part because of the yellow fever epidemics in the 1870s, their children were born and raised in New York City. She and her sister Beatrice were among their offspring. Florence's higher education included attendance at a "normal school" subsequently incorporated into Hunter College.

Florence (née Lowenstein) Marshall married Louis Marshall in New York City on May 6, 1895; he was 16 years her senior. Samuel Untermyer,[1] the bride's second cousin, was a partner in the law firm her husband had earlier joined. Florence was eight when her own mother died. The Marshall/ Lowenstein marriage produced four children. Ruth, their only daughter, was just 13 when Florence Marshall died at age 37 (Silver, p. 30).

A paper subtitled "A Case Study of Guggenheimer, Untermyer & Marshall of New York City and the Predecessor Partnerships" focused upon the marketing of American legal services over an era of 6½-decades be- ginning some 1⅔ centuries ago. The author's central theme was a "belief of the WASP legal establishment that the law was a gentlemen's profession; by the late 19th century changes in the structure of the American economy had profoundly altered the nature of the profession" (Dawkins, 2013, p. 239). Said author alleged in his text for "The Marketing of Legal in the United States, 1855-1912" that Samuel Untermyer,[2] a partner in the subject law firm, purportedly relished an "...on-going feud with [international banker] J. P. Morgan, Sr. who appears to have sought to exclude Untermyer from WASP society" (p. 254).

Over the two decades of Florence Marshall's marriage, no spousal insights about her husband's possible thinking about an American-oriented "Judaism of the future" are readily discernible. In an ancillary context, Rabbi Judah L. Magnes—the husband of her younger sister, Beatrice (née Lowenstein) Magnes—once headed Temple Emanu-El in New York City before ultimately migrating to the West Coast and undertaking other national and international missions.

---

[1] Samuel Untermyer, the son of a Confederate Army officer born in Lynchburg in the Old South, was a lifelong member of the Democratic Party while Marshall was a lifelong member of the Republican Party. Untermyer's behind-the-scenes role in supporting Louis D. Brandeis's nomination to the U.S. Supreme Court by fellow Virginian [Thomas] Woodrow Wilson has often been overlooked. Prof. Felix Adler first met future Pres. Wilson in the early 1890s when Wilson attended Adler's Plymouth Summer School of Applied Ethics in Massachusetts and again at the White House on Feb. 2, 1914, when Adler urged the Pres. "to heed the national conscience" (Lifshitz, p. 61) by quashing proposed laws condoning the continuation of unregulated child labor.

[2] He served as president of the Palestine Foundation after Marshall succeeded him as former firm's managing partner.

5. Diverging Conceptualizations of an American "Judaism of the Future"

Meanwhile, let us return to Felix Adler's Sabbath address on Oct. 11, 1873 at Temple Emanu-El in New York City in which he alluded to his nascent credo envisioning a "Judaism for the future." Attempting to juxtapose Louis Marshall's concepts about the aspirations of Jews *vis-à-vis* Felix's related foresights is complicated. The ensuing passage, excerpted from a 1914 lecture given by Louis Marshall in Syracuse, speaks for itself:

> "Keep out of the melting pot," Marshall warned his audience in speaking about *The Melting Pot*, a book by Israel Zangwill [a play staged in 1908]...Keep unto yourselves that which made Israel of old a priest[ly] people. He [Zangwill] would pour the gold, the silver, the zinc, copper, lead [and] iron all into one pot and melt them. When he got through, he would have a mixture but no virtues. It would be too cheap for jewelry, it could not replace silver, it would be too brittle to replace iron and not docile enough for copper..." (reported in the Nov. 7, 1914 issue of the *Syracuse Post-Standard*).

Excerpted from Marshall's correspondence addressed to a "dissatisfied" rabbinical aspirant (see Appendix III) is a prescient passage about Adler's innovative teachings:

> "The program you have marked out for yourself does not appeal to me as a practical one, or conducive to the training of a Jewish rabbi. The pursuit of Hebrew studies at Columbia University, attendance on such classes at the Seminary which you may deem valuable, the taking of a few courses in the Union Theological Seminary, and study under Dr. Felix Adler is a rather eclectic course of study. To me it is rather startling, and partakes of the nature of an electrical toy consisting of a disc divided into many colors which, when rapidly revolved, becomes entirely colorless. You might be able to manufacture a new religion of your own by that method, but it will not be Judaism. Nor do I believe that it would enable you to accomplish the earnest ambitions which you entertain and which I highly respect" (Marshall, 1928a, p. 869).[1]

It is understandable why Marshall took issue with the universalist tenor of Prof. Adler's credo predicated upon "purist" and idealistic attitudes about mankind's fundamental morality. For him, the *zeitgeist* of such a Judaism would devolve into an "entirely colorless" faith.

---

[1] Although editor Charles Reznikoff furnished transcripts of Marshall's lengthy communications with the "dissatisfied" rabbinical aspirant, another author "outed" this unnamed person as one Eugene Lehman, who apparently had distinguished himself as an undergraduate at Yale University prior to becoming "one of America's first Rhodes Scholars to study at Oxford, whereupon he "… quickly became disenchanted with the Jewish Theological Seminary" (Silver, pp. 56-58).

6. Of Nativism and Antisemitism

White later achieved renown as American ambassador to Russia and then Germany. He assisted American envoy to Russia T. H. Seymour as his diplomatic *attaché* and translator while abroad in 1854-1855. Russia had been a signatory of the United States Treaty of 1832 (the Buchanan Treaty), which was enacted in the year of Amb. White's birth. At the time, no one anticipated that the terms of such legislation were susceptible to future discrimination against Jewish citizens carrying an American passport.

During the intervening quarter-century between Amb. White's postings in Russia, a heightened cycle of pogroms dehumanized Jewish existence in areas commonly known as the Pale of Jewish Settlement (Leonard, pp. 6-26). Such pogroms blocked the flow of alien refugees to the United States. The "American minister to Russia [White] had argued that the admission of East European Jews [to the United States] should be regulated" (Silver, p. 127). Marshall had always opposed an American foreign policy condoning Russian discrimination against Jews by prohibiting issuance of travel visas to them.

Such nativist laws served to stoke the simmering issue of American anti-immigration campaigns via the imposition quota systems that both restricted Jews and barred Asians as well as requiring literacy tests. Marshall lobbied for federal "open immigration" policies while advocating on behalf of local Americanization leagues that were supportive of applications for citizenship.[1] He had always opposed efforts to have the U.S. Census Bureau list Jews as a racial category. His unceasing efforts, as an international advocate for downtrodden *landsmen* trapped in Russia's Pale of Jewish Settlement, gained impetus as a burgeoning movement.

A mass meeting sponsored by the National Citizens Committee was held at Carnegie Hall in New York City on Dec. 6, 1911. Former Amb. to Russia White was heralded as one of the keynote speakers. Sentiments overwhelmingly favored the validation of American passports held by Jews[2] while eliminating impediments against Jewish migration from Russia to America.[3] Amb. White had earlier unsuccessfully urged that the dispute be submitted for arbitration at an international tribunal at The

Hague in Holland. Jewish migration from Russia to America eventually became regulated by a quota system under the U.S. Immigration Act of 1924, along with legislation barring Asians.

---

[1] See Ginsburg (2019).

[2] Before enactment of the 1907 Burnett-Dillingham bill, Marshall led his futile campaign to quash Amb. White's bias toward regulating emigration to the United States.

[3] As president of the American Jewish Committee, Marshall wrote His Holiness Pope Benedict XV on Dec. 30, 1915 seeking his humanitarian intervention in alleviating persecution of "The Jews in the Eastern War Zone." In his epic efforts opposing enactment of the U.S. Immigration Act of 1924, Marshall mobilized the Yiddish-language press as a metaphorical "political bill-board" (Rischin, 1962, p. 231), both here and abroad.

7. A "Genteel" *Détente?*

Notably, the Marshall progeny and several children of the expanded Adler clan were educated at the pre-collegiate Fieldston School sponsored by the Ethical Culture Society in Manhattan, where Felix Adler had been its founding patron and rector (a position reminiscent of an Anglican academy's headmaster).

Certain insights voiced by the widowed Helen Adler about her deceased husband and mother-in-law seem historically significant. In her first-person reminiscences, she wrote:

"He [Felix] started as a quite young man in his early twenties a course of innovations in public and social work that led to the first Free Kindergarten in the United States [as well as] to the first district nursing service by trained nurses. Then came improved tenements and many other reforms, a long career of educational pioneering and child training..." (H. Adler, 1939, p. 2).

Marshall, in the words of one biographer, "complained about Tammany [Hall], in exchanges with Felix Adler, the founder of the Ethical Cultural Society...who had publicly lauded [Mayor Seth] Low as "the Last best hope of earth" (Silver, p. 42). He continued by declaring to Adler that "I am and always have been a Republican and have no sympathy with Tammany Hall" *(ibid.,* p. 548, fn. 57).

It seems plausible, in retrospect, that Marshall had merely been cautioning Adler about risking further alliances with Mayor Low's deputized police chief. According to a newspaper account published on Apr. 23, 1900:

"Felix Adler, founder of the nonsectarian Society for Ethical Culture described in 1900 how Police Chief William S. Devery whispered in his ear, "It's just you Jews" who were responsible in the 'bad moral conditions in the city' (Silver, p. 43). Speaking before eight hundred people of an anti-vice rally at the Eldridge Synagogue, Adler's words were immediately drowned in an outburst of angry shouts. Devery and others' claims had a direct effect upon the way Jews increasingly identified their defamers as 'Anglo-Saxons' or 'Yankees'..." (Ribak, p. 11, fn. 38).

8. "Homes Away from Home" Atop Mountain Greenery

Felix Adler was one of the early pioneers in Keene Valley at Beede's in upstate New York (H. Adler, 1939, p. 1). "Beede's" refers to the Beede House built in 1876 as a way station for boarders in St. Huberts, N.Y., in the high peaks of the Adirondack Mountains. It was named after the patron saint of hunted deer.

According to home-grown native historian Weston:
> "Teachers, writers, and philosophers, several of them friends of Ralph Waldo Emerson or Mark Twain, came to the area. The most noted were William James, Felix Adler, and Thomas Davidson (all of whom brought followers or disciples), as well as Charles Dudley Warner. These professionals had long vacations and, once the arduous journey was made, usually stayed for two or three months. Summer visitors were not tourists as we think of transients today" (p. 12).

The respective sojourns of the extended Adler family in the Adirondacks became and remain indelible. Many became summer-long *habitués*.[1] Felix had been a principal progenitor of the Adirondack Trail Improvement Society in 1897. A hiking trail leading from the nearby Ausable Club had long been called the Felix Adler Hiking Trail. A successor entity, the Adirondack Mountain Club, was founded in 1922 (Hopsicker, p. 210). Another trail, leading to the summit of Noonmark Mountain, came to honor Henry L. Stimson,[2] who served as Secretary of War in World War I and World War II. A further trail was duly named after William James.

Felix and Helen must have been captivated by the poetry of Ralph Waldo Emerson. They gave the middle name Waldo to their eldest son.[3] As one biographer observed, Felix "was and remained far more Emersonian than he knew or cared to admit" (Guttchen, p. 24). Late in life, his widow Helen Adler characterized their familial *milieu* as "truly an example of Emersonian 'plain living and high thinking'" H. Adler, 1939, p. 3).

A group of young Boston physicians—James J. Putnam, Charles P.

Putnam, Henry P. Bowditch and William James—had earlier purchased another tract of Beede family-owned farmland. They gradually developed a summer colony for their families and guests which came to be known as the Putnam Camp.[4] The nearby Glenmore School for Cultural Sciences founded by Thomas Davidson in 1889 at East Hill (about 10 miles north of St. Huberts) had a profound influence on the philosophical thinking of James (Weston, p. 22). William James soon sold his quarter interest in the Putnam Camp to James J. Putnam.

The unimproved acreage purchased at St. Huberts by Adler in 1882 was situated 24 miles southeast of the 500-acre waterfront where Marshall and his associates had lodges built within a commonly owned tract dubbed Knollwood along the shores of Lower Saranac Lake in 1899. In effect, they could experience the beauty and tranquility of the wilderness devoid of antisemitism without fouling their pristine and regulated environment.

At first glance, when Adler and Marshall independently established their homes away from home astride the Adirondack Mountains, the linkages between their two extended families in nearby sylvan retreats may seem contrived. For historical context, one may harken back to the national *cause célèbre* precipitated on June 13, 1877, when former Judge Henry Hilton, then manager of the Grand Union Hotel in Saratoga Springs *(New York Times,* 1877b), denied entry to Joseph Seligman (see Chapter 1 for his role as Felix Adler's initial benefactor) and his entourage.[5] They had previously vacationed at the resort without any discrimination triggered by their distinction as readily identifiable "Israelites." Ten days later, an investigative journalist for the *New York Times* wrote a piece headlined "How Philadelphia Stands" in which he said that "a Philadelphia [the City of Brotherly Love] hotel executive noted that the 'money of an Israelite is as good as that of a full-fledged Jew'..."

By 1906, a senior member of the New York State Board of Regents, Melvil Dewey (the inventor of the Dewey Decimal System for library classifications) was a prominent public official. He had used official stationery from his governmental department to distribute circulars of the private Lake Placid Club in which Jews were characterized as "members of an undesirable and obnoxious group" (Wise, pp. 187-188). Marshall protested to the governor about Dewey's behavior and demanded his removal from office "upon the ground of discriminatory prejudice against a large element of the citizenry of the state of New York." So effective and vigorous were Marshall's allegations about Dewey's quasi-official misfeasance that he was compelled to resign his position as a public official.

The Dearborn Independent, owned by industrialist Henry Ford, had a history of publishing virulent antisemitic diatribes. On June 3, 1920, Ford approved a telegram apologizing for his newspaper's habit of disseminating bogus propaganda about an alleged "Jewish diabolic threat to take over the world." It has been said that the telegram was actually ghost-written by Marshall in Ford's name. If so, Marshall seemed amenable to lessening Gentile backlash by not succumbing to his own adversarial proclivities.

Meanwhile, Russell M. L. Carson, an avid mountain-climber, conservationist and member of the Adirondack Mountain Club, compiled and wrote an Adirondack guide entitled *Peaks and People of the Adirondacks* published by the Adirondack Mountain Club in 1927. In it, according to Hopsicker, Carson proposed to "tell the how, when, and why" about the names of the 46 Adirondack peaks rising 4,000 feet or higher "about which but very little has ever been known." In Hopsicker's further words:

> "While mountaineers quickly adopted *Peaks and People* in the Adirondacks as their 'go-to' reference for the high peaks, it was the names [Carlson] gave to those peaks that spawned an immediate rebuke from Theodore Van Wyck Anthony…Specifically, Anthony protests the naming of Mount Marshall after George and Robert [hereafter affectionately known as 'Bob'] Marshall whom Carson describes as valuable contributors 'to the cause of mountaineering in the Adirondacks.' Anthony tinged the matter with racist over-tones acknowledging that some of his 'enemies'…would accuse him of religious prejudice since Robert[7] and George Marshall are Hebrews.[6] While Anthony claims no such prejudice in his challenge [to Carson's 'assumption of authority' of giving names to natural monuments to 'any man now living'],[7] the end of his letter implies otherwise when he admits to a pro-Gentile leaning on all points of controversy… and if that be a religious prejudice,[8] make the most of it" (Hopsicker, p. 211).

The full text of the cited article by Hopsicker (p. 205) is entitled " 'No Hebrews Allowed': How the 1932 Lake Placid Winter Olympic Games Survived the 'Restricted' Adirondack Culture, 1877-1932." It appeared in the *Journal of Sport History.* A subheading entitled "The Adirondack's Flagship for Bigotry: The Lake Placid Club" characterized the retreat, founded in 1895, as "an efficient WASP's nest" (p. 208) whose goal was to "build a community wealthy Jews would covet but could not join"[9] (p. 209).

[1] Helen's next-oldest Goldmark sister, Pauline Dorothea, graduated from Bryn Mawr College in 1896, as her younger Goldmark sister Josephine Clara had done in 1898. Pauline Goldmark, in the company of her nephew, 14-year-old Waldo Adler, initially crossed paths with William James a half-mile from the Putnam Camp near the St. Huberts summer home of the Adler couple in 1895 (Simon, 1996, p. 177). He was then 53 years old and she was 21. Pauline was about to begin her final year as an undergraduate biology major; she was athletic with expertise as a naturalist. Outfitted in boys' breeches, she "climbs like a monkey," James once wrote. Some literary sleuths have concluded—predicated on the collective correspondence of William James and Pauline Goldmark—that the affectionate relationship they developed over the succeeding 15 years may have been romantic in nature (Simon, pp., 172-198; Rosenzweig, pp. 182-197). See also *The Religion of Democracy: Seven Liberals and the American Moral Tradition* (Kittelstrom, 2015), in which the author alluded to the resentment of the wife of William James to Pauline Goldmark, his hiking companion (p. 158). The author likewise noted that in the 1890s, James "...boycotted the Wil[l]ey House, a grand country hotel that closed its doors to Jews..." *(ibid.,* p. 244).

[2] Pres. F.D. Roosevelt insisted that nothing could be done to extricate death-sentenced Jews from Nazi Germany except to win World War II. Secretary of War Henry L. Stimson vigorously opposed the creation of a temporary haven to shelter Jewish refugees at Fort Ontario in Oswego, N.Y., because they "...were 'unassimilable' and would undermine the purity of America's 'racial stock'..." (Medoff, 2019, p. 221).

[3] He graduated from the University of the South at Sewanee in Tennessee.

[4] The architect of this conglomeration was Dr. Edward Emerson, the son of Ralph Waldo Emerson (Gifford, 1972, p. 28). Sigmund Freud, Carl G. Jung and Sándor Ferenczi were among their foreign guests.

[5] A son, Edwin R. A. Seligman, was then an adolescent. He later became an economics Prof. at Columbia University and an early owner of a Lake Placid shorefront lot that the Lake Placid Club (a private organization founded and headed by Melvil Dewey) had previously aspired to own. For 26 years, the junior Seligman served as Pres. of the Lake Placid Shore Owners' Association (Tatham, pp. 22 & 26). Among the Jewish-born members of the organization were a cousin, Florine Stettheimer, at Calumet Lodge on Moose Island, as well as Rabbi Stephen S. Wise at Buck Island (pp. 6 & 21). It is implausible to suggest that any of them could then have qualified as a candidate for membership at the private club. Prior to the turn of the 19th century and thereafter, the future Rabbi Stephen S. Wise was a regular summer devotee of "Thomas Davidson, a Scottish immigrant and liberal philosopher, who nurtured Wise's inclination to see modern questions through Judaism's moral teachings" (Storch, 2017, p.

401). At his Adirondacks retreat, Davidson "hosted the voluntary and eclectic Glenmore School for the Culture Sciences, as well as friends and scholars such as William James, Charlotte Perkins Gilman, Thomas Dewey, and Wise, who came to hike, recite poetry, read, write and openly discuss and debate ideas. Davidson's friendship connected Wise to an intellectual and political world that transcended Judaism but upheld its prophetic tradition, which encourages speaking moral truths regardless of how unpopular the truths may be. Davidson predicted that Wise would devise a twentieth century Judaism fitted to the needs of the present day…" *(ibid.).* As a young adult, the future Louise (née Waterman) Wise "embraced Felix Adler's Ethical Culture Movement, and at Adler's suggestion, she began working in the city's settlement houses and taught art to youth who lived in the tenements" *(ibid.,* p. 405).

[6] Beginning at 3:30 a.m. on July 15, 1932, Bob, armed with flashlights, "ascended fourteen peaks and a total of 13,600 feet in one day" within the Adirondack range of mountains (Weber, 2003, p. 146). At 10:10 p.m. that night, he descended from the summit of Mount Jo to the "Adirondack Loj" where he received "a warm reception and Elise Untermyer gave him a delicious warm supper." Bob was a charter member of what became known as the 46ers Club. It was restricted to those who, like his brother George, had climbed all 46 Adirondack high peaks (mountains taller than 4,000 feet). He later became a collegiate cross-country and lacrosse competitor at Syracuse University (Glover, 1986, p. 53) as well as a marathon mountain-climber and Arctic explorer. Although Bob identified himself as a liberal Socialist and godless Jew, there is a poignant passage he authored about his Jewishness. Biographer Glover's third-hand version speaks for itself: "On Yom Kippur, September 1925, however, Marshall took an unusually short hike. Yom Kippur, the Day of Atonement on the Jewish calendar, is a time for quiet reflection. So Marshall went out that morning [in the "Coeur d'Alene National Forest"] to be alone and to think…For three hours he sat on a rock contemplating the scene, getting up at intervals to walk a short way down the trail. When the day was over he compared this method of reflection with the manner he would have observed Yom Kippur back in New York. Here in the woods, he found "there is no wandering of thoughts…to the less frivolous subjects of pine reproduction or the political situation." On the other hand, he was "forced to confess" that *"in Temple…it in the past been impossible to banish such thoughts from my mind and that, at best, fasting, hard seats and dull sermons are not conducive to deep thought. Therefore, I feel that my celebration of Yom Kippur, though unorthodox, was very profitable."* The woods in other words were Marshall's temple" (pp. 79-81, with lines underlined presumably in Bob's own handwriting). See R. Marshall for the likely unpaginated and unpublished first-person autobiographical source.

[7] A former name for the disputed "high peak" in question had been Mt. Dix. Unmentioned by Hopsicker is the fact that the American speed skater Irving Jaffe won two Olympic gold medals at the same winter Olympic games for which he was later inducted into the International Jewish Sports Hall of Fame.

[8] "While there has been a good deal written about the Jewish community's protest against the participation of the United States in the 1936 'Nazi Games,' scholars have largely missed how similar antisemitic sentiment affected the 1932 Lake Placid winter Olympic games" (Hopsicker, p. 205). Even more egregious is a hate letter about Louis Marshall authored by the same disgruntled member of the Adirondack Mountain Club to another co-member (T. V. W. Anthony to J. Apperson, May 27, 1928): "Our friend, Louis Marshall, has effectively disguised his race by assuming his present name. I believe that I [Anthony, p. 90] am entitled to pull off the disguise. If his name was Marshallowitski, or Guggenheimer, or Untermyer it would speak for itself. He is trying to 'get away' with his '100% Americanism' by disguising his race under the most honored name in American jurisprudence" (presumably Chief Justice "John Marshall" of the Supreme Court of the United States of America).

[9] On his 16th birthday, Moses A. Cohen (1884-1961), disembarked as a steerage *émigré* from a transatlantic steamship in New York City. He was posthumously profiled as "a penniless boy from Russia who became an American capitalist in the Adirondacks" (Wessels, p. 31). In *Moses Cohen—Peddler to Capitalist:An Adirondack Pioneer Merchant,* it was said that he literally lugged the capital for his future home improvement venture "upon his own back" *(ibid.).* His mother had reputedly "wanted him to become a rabbi" *(ibid.,* p. 6). Older brother David had preceded him during the during the *fin de siècle* decade of the 19th century. He had begun to establish himself as a struggling entrepreneur of a local hardware store d/b/a D. Cohen & Sons in the hamlet of Bloomingdale, N. Y. in Essex County. Ultimately, they helped found the first synagogue in the Adirondacks at Tupper Lake, N. Y. Along the way, both became successful retail merchants. Neither he nor Moses was conversant in English; Yiddish was their only language. A solitary occupation remained for Moses: "…put a pack upon his back and peddle, going from farm to farm, village to village, over the hills and through the woods to wherever there was a dwelling to be found and there to make friends and make a sale. His brother gave him this advice: 'If you see a chimney, there is a house. Look for the door and if a woman comes to meet you, try and sell her something and get lodging for the night if it be near dusk'… The pack that they carried was unique; the pack was in reality two packs. The main pack was made out of ticking, reached from the shoulders down to the calves of their legs and was packed with the heavy items for trade, such as underwear for men, women and children; the red and white checkered tablecloths, the ladies' wrappers; these latter two items were great sellers; men's shirts, women's underwear and other unmentionables and the children's wear. There was another pack, a sort of valise that was strapped around their middle which carried the notions such as elastic by the yard, buttons, men's and women's stockings, threads, needle and pins, and other items. The larger pack also carried some small tinware. The two packs would weigh up to 80 or 100 lbs… The pack cost from \$16.00 to \$30.00, depending upon what was in the pack… It took about three weeks to walk [his foot-route]… over hill and dale, often wading through mud up to his knees…" (pp.

8-9). Moses graduated to "a horse and cart" *(ibid.,* p. 31) by the time he launched his thriving hardware enterprise and was celebrated as "Mr. Old Forge" *(ibid.,* p. 25). The Enchanted Forest Water Safari amusement park in Old Forge, N.Y., was the brainchild of Moses's son Richard Cohen. Awaiting a future historiography beyond the scope of this side trip is the story of Henry Minoru a/k/a "Hank" Kashiwa and members of his extended family who succeeded the descendants of the Cohen family as leading merchant-pioneers in Old Forge. For commentary about seasonal vacationers from Montreal and elsewhere, see "The Shul at Loon Lake" by Ruth R. Wisse (2009). It begins: "The Loon Lake Jewish Center, about two-thirds of the way between Plattsburgh and Saranac Lake, New York, is a log cabin, a former hunting lodge, consisting of one large square room that serves as a sanctuary" (p. 38).

9. Historical Legacies

The mid-19th century European thinking of revolutionist émigré J. J. Goldmark had been waning in America.[1] Meanwhile, at the 1894 New York State Constitutional Convention, Marshall had begun his quest to formulate conservation legislation to forever protect the Adirondack wilderness. He sponsored state laws creating the College of Forestry (now known as the New York State College of Environmental Sciences and Forestry) in Syracuse. He became a founding trustee of the *Association for the Protection of the Adirondack Wilderness.* By the beginning of the ensuing century, the then-deceased Goldmark's son Henry was overseeing engineering plans for the hydraulic locks at the Panama Canal. His sister, Alice (née Goldmark) Brandeis, also a surviving offspring of Goldmark, provided funding along with her husband for the criminal defenses of Sacco and Vanzetti as well as a physical refuge for Rosina Sacco and her children from the press in a home Brandeis owned (Urofsky, p. 643). Pauline and Josephine Goldmark continued to flourish as acclaimed social activists and authors (P. Goldmark; J. C. Goldmark).

Meanwhile, the elder Marshall's lifelong political leanings were centered with the Republican Party. His international endeavors championing the Jewish people were reaching an apex. His wife, Florence (née Lowenstein) Marshall, though 17 years his junior, predeceased him in 1916. Her death when the younger sons were adolescents and young adults must have been heartbreaking. Older son James served in World War I and then practiced law in New York City, where he supported Republican Mayor Fiorello H. LaGuardia. Louis Marshall died suddenly on Sept. 11, 1929 in Zurich.

Although the philosophic trajectories espoused by Adler's innovative movement may have been spreading internationally, some Jewish-American proponents seemed stalwart in resisting the thrust of his programs to promote the Ethical Culture Society as a plausibly corrective antidote to other quasi-religious/doctrinaire callings. The causes he had founded and inspired were gradually becoming more tenuous as the World War I era receded.

The lives of the elder Marshall and Adler obviously overlapped. Nevertheless, it seems useful to contrast the eventual philosophic outlooks of the two youngest lads with those of Adler in his capacity as rector. Adler was highly critical of socialism, insisting that the "all men were created equal" mantra was fallible because of the overriding perniciousness of mankind's innate greed.[2] Neither Bob nor George Marshall came to regard ethical culture as their religion. During their respective adult lives, they attained doctorates in plant physiology and economics. Bob, for one, eventually came to consider himself a "God-less Jew." He served as secretary of the Washington branch of the *American Civil Liberties Union.* The distribution of his inherited share of the family's fortune was specifically calculated to support humanitarian causes predicated on social equality.

Bob[3] and George became ardent conservationists in promoting Adirondack causes. After their father's death during the early throes of the Great Depression, both became vociferously critical of certain New Deal projects in which they had participated. By mid-20th century, George was summoned before the House Committee on Un-American Activities and exercised his Fifth Amendment right in refusing to testify, whereupon he was cited for contempt of Congress and served three months in federal prison, according to a June 18, 2000 account in the *New York Times.*

---

[1] The first name of daughter Josephine Clara Goldmark embodied the feminized version of her father's name. She eulogized him in *Pilgrims of '48: One Man's Part in the Austrian Revolution of 1848 and a Family Migration to America* (1930).

[2] Adler apparently articulated his excerpted opinion in a column published in a Jan. 28, 1895 issue of the *New York Times.*

[3] Son Bob had been a collegiate cross-country and lacrosse competitor (Glover, p. 53) as well as a marathon mountain-climber and Arctic explorer. While he had reputedly been top scorer in a civil service examination, his progression through the U.S. Forestry Service was not without controversy as a conservationist. In his capacity as director of the Indian Forest Service, he became a protectionist for the rights of all Native Americans; he seemed to relish his role as a champion of indigenous cultures. "In 1933 [Bob] began a battle of cultures as well as the war over the wilderness. After [his designation as] Director of the Indian Forest Service he went on to fight for the rights of native Americans... His vision for the recreation areas of National Parks included every race, sex, religion and creed... [for him, commercial] resorts represented a plethora of problems in [his] eyes; not only were they a potential hazard to the environment, they

directly conflicted with his Civil Rights view by banning minorities." Although his parents were mainly known for their support of Jewish-oriented causes, their later support of civil rights grew beyond just Jewish causes to eventually include Roman Catholics, Native Americans, Japanese, African-Americans and socialists.

10. An Adler/Goldmark Familial Luminary: The Hon. Louis D. Brandeis

We return to Aug. 26, 1890, when Louis D. Brandeis, a second cousin of Alice Goldmark, arrived at St. Huberts on the written invitation of his future wife Alice (Helen's sister). Both were American-born, though many of the senior members of their intertwined extended families were Jewish immigrants from Europe. Several had lived in Kentucky, Indiana, Massachusetts and New York. Alice and her brother Henry had fortuitously encountered Brandeis in St. Louis earlier in the year. Both men had been acquainted as Harvard University graduates. Louis became a lawyer; he "probably remembered Alice [his future wife] as a little girl, or at most a teen-ager" (Urofsky, p. 106). They married in New York City on Mar. 23, 1891. Officiating at the wedding was Dr. Felix Adler. Brandeis had already celebrated his 34th birthday; Alice was a decade younger.

Gentile-oriented thinking had been deeply embedded within the humanist/ naturalistic philosophies dominated by Ralph Waldo Emerson and William James as the 19th century began to wane. Unfolding across the Atlantic Ocean were the aftereffects of two Jewish-rooted concerns—the Dreyfus affair and the first World Zionist Congress. While attending meetings in Switzerland for that conference, Marshall[1] and Albert Einstein began an enduring friendship.

On June 1, 1916, Pres. Woodrow Wilson's nominee Brandeis was sworn in as Justice of the Supreme Court. At a White House meeting on Aug. 8, 1916, Wilson enlisted the assistance of Brandeis to head an extrajudicial three-man delegation to "meet with a similar group named by the Mexican government to settle differences that brought the two nations close to war" (ibid., pp. 494-495). As the most junior member of the Court, Brandeis headed north to the summer home of Chief Justice Edward D. White at Lake Placid to seek his assent for such participation.

However, his mission proved unproductive. He then wrote to Alice (née Goldmark) Brandeis about his reaction to the people at Lake Placid, whom he termed "depressive in the extreme." His biographer Urofsky wrote:
 "The only redeeming encounter, other than with the chief jus-

tice, had been with a Zionist he met at the train who recognized him. 'I never felt more the chasm between me & the prosperous gentility'...and 'it was a wondrous relief to find *one of my own people*'...*"* [emphasis added] *(ibid.).*

Still sensitive after the attacks made on him during the confirmation fight, Brandeis could not have ignored the fact that in Lake Placid, as in many other resort areas, many hotels refused to take Jews as guests.[2]

Rabbi and fellow Zionist Stephen S. Wise could have offered some solace for the upset jurist had he been in residence at his retreat along the shores of Lake Placid. Or Brandeis may have welcomed a respite, a mere few miles distant, at the summer home of his sister-in-law's family. Perhaps he spared himself the prospect of facing a hypothetical question: "Is my outspokenly anti-Zionist brother-in-law still 'one of my people?'"

Marshall was a mere month younger than Brandeis. By this time, each had achieved national renown as leading lawyers and had been instrumental in reaching the Marshall Compromise ending the New York City Cloakmakers' Strike[3] involving industrial safety, among many other issues, for over 50,000 workers.

---

[1] Albert Einstein (1879-1955), who had often been a guest of the Marshall family, was vacationing at Knollwood when he first received word that the atomic bomb had devastated Hiroshima.

[2] Future researchers on antisemitism in the Adirondack Mountains are urged to examine further detailed historical facts in re: Felix Adler, members of his extended family (wife, brother, daughter, son, nieces, nephews *et al). Familiarity with Two Adirondack Hamlets in History: Keene and Keene Valley,* edited by Richard Plunz (1999), is indispensable. His contextual profiles amplify many prescient insights about Felix's interrelationships with fellow philosophers, psychologist William James and others. See also fns. 79 *(ibid.,* p. 262), 80 *(ibid.,* p. 262) and 182 *(ibid.,* p. 266) amongst others.

[3] "Marshall offered special thanks to Brandeis, whom he saw as a true hero" (Greenwald, p. 327).

11. Ascertainable Probate Data[1] for Specific Distributees and Transgenerational Legatees

Instead of attempting to document how Jews in America were inclined to forsake their Biblical identities or cling to Old World cultures, suffice it to observe that the credo of Adler's Ethical Culture movement inspired its devotees to distinguish themselves by social concerns and good deeds.

Both the senior Adler and Marshall had been leaders of several activist movements advocating for American civil rights causes. Adler had ascended the ranks of academia to become a full professor at Columbia University. In contrast, a eulogist for Marshall wrote: "Although not a college graduate, he educated himself to such a degree that any such graduate would envy… (H. Stern, p. 115).

It is not known whether any members of the respective extended Adler/Goldmark families ever accessed possible probate or Surrogate's Court records related to their respective next of kin. Horace L. Friess, Felix's disciple and executor, married daughter Eleanor before he became privy to the Adler family's literary *œuvre*. A compendium of such data entitled *Felix Adler and Ethical Culture: Memories and Studies* was edited by Fania Weingartner (1981). Just as Adler apparently designated a son-in-law as the testamentary and *de facto* guardian of his so-called "spiritual" legacy, so too may one infer the appearance of possible nepotism in favor of Jacob Billikopf (Marshall's Lithuanian-born son-in-law)[2] prior to and after the early death of his wife Ruth (née Marshall) Billikopf.[3]

The senior Billikopf became an outspoken crusader for social equality. Along the way, he was appointed to the Kansas City Board of Pardons and Parole. He ultimately came to head an arbitration board in the men's apparel industry in New York City (see more than 400 of his arbitration awards catalogued in Collection #5110 at the Kheel Center for Labor-Management Documentation and Archives at the Cornell University Library in Ithaca, N.Y.). He also headed an arbitration panel for the ladies' garment industry in Philadelphia. Among other distinctions, he also served as an impartial chairman of the Federal Regional Labor Board in Washington, D.C., where he became a trustee of Howard University. Like his father-in-law,[4] he was awarded an honorary academic degree (LL.D.) by the University of Richmond.

Louis Marshall's last will and testament dated Mar. 19, 1921 was filed in October 1929 in the Surrogate's Court of the borough of Manhattan. The estimated value of its assets was $5 million, and a tenth of the residuary estate was earmarked for enumerated charitable beneficiaries.[5] The bulk of the senior Marshall's estate devolved to his four children. A generation later, after Bob's death in 1939, his gross estate before taxes amounted to $1,534,070 (Glover, p. 272). Adirondack guide Herbert Clark, a second father figure to Marshall, received a bequest of $3,000. Under further terms of the will, tripartite trusts were established. Each segment provided for the creation of a charitable entity to foster educational goals for "the development and organization of unions of persons and the promotion of an economic system in the United States based upon the theory of production for use and not-for-profit;" to safeguard civil liberties in the United States; and to fund the creation of a "wilderness movement."

Perhaps unbeknownst to Billikopf, his son David Marshall Billikopf (1926-2018), soon after his father's death came to identify himself as a follower of the Roman Catholic faith albeit an ethnic Jew.[6] The son, a mature Harvard University graduate, had initially met the woman whom he was to wed on a transatlantic voyage when he received a cable notifying him of his father's demise. The then-parentless Billikopf son relocated to Chile (where she resided) to court her. In 1973,[7] he authored a treatise entitled *The Exercise of Judicial Power, 1789-1864.* A contemporary first cousin, Jonathan Marshall (1924-2008), an Arizona publisher, became a member of the Democratic Party and was defeated in a race for the U.S. Senate by Republican Barry Goldwater.

---

[1] Authoritative biographical publications such as *A Wilderness Original* (Glover, 1986) have been cited as such second-hand sources.

[2] Four analogous samples of pertinent correspondence quoted and cited in Appendix II: [*Per* 6/7/1923 letter at pp. 911-913 (LM/*CR*)]; [*Per* 10/18/1924 letter at pp. 883-887 (LM/*CR*)]; [*Per* 4/10/1926 letter at pp. 228-234 (LM/*CR*)]; [*Per* 2/19/1929 letter at pp. 1145-1146 (LM/*CR*)].

[3] Ruth was 16 years younger than her husband Jacob when they married. Their union may serve to highlight "associational networks" within the Adler/Goldmark and Marshall/Lowenstein families beyond the walls of Adler's Fieldston School. Jacob Billikopf had been a leader of Jewish communal causes in Missouri and

elsewhere. In Kansas City, he mentored Helen Ross, who graduated from the University of Missouri in 1911 and augmented her income as a public school teacher by coaching immigrants in English at a local Jewish night school. The Jacob Billikopf/Ruth Marshall couple settled in Philadelphia, as did Helen Ross for her graduate studies at Bryn Mawr College. She not only credited Billikopf's tutelage for her interest in social work but also praised "the famous Goldmark sisters" (Thompson, pp. 166-167). While qualifying as a psychoanalyst, Ross became a long-time confidant, colleague and friend of Anna Freud. Based in Chicago, Ross was pivotal in securing funding from the Marshall Field Foundation for Anna Freud's research sponsored at London's Hampstead Clinic. She and her brother Charles Ross (Pres. H. S. Truman's press chief) were native-born Missourians hailing from the city of Independence. It behooves us to at least mention the Adler/Goldmark linkages while factoring possible gender-oriented predilections predating the emergence of women's emancipation. Felix's niece Hetty Goldman (see Chapter 1, endnote 1), like her prestigious uncle Felix and Goldmark cousins, distinguished herself as a prestigious academician. With degrees from Bryn Mawr College and a doctorate from Radcliffe College, she became the first woman faculty member at the Institute for Advanced Study in Princeton. According to an account published in the *New York Times* on June 30, 1919, she witnessed "starvation and destruction among the Jews of Rumania, Bulgaria, Greece and Serbs [as] an agent of the Joint Distribution Committee of the American Funds for Jewish War Sufferers."

[4] After Marshall served as a Syracuse University trustee beginning in 1910, he was not averse to voicing his differences with the very institution that had awarded him the LL.D. *honoris causa* academic distinction in 1913. His unsuccessful Reply Brief on Appeal in opposition to the Bill of Impeachment filed against then-sitting New York Governor William L. Sulzer bore the imprimatur "Louis Marshall, LL.D.," illustrating an example of when a prominent member of the Republican Party was retained to defend the Democratic Party's political leader.

[5] The library at the Syracuse University College of Law was among the fractional-income beneficiaries of the testator's charitable residuary trust.

[6] One of Jacob Billikopf's grandsons identified himself as a devotee of the Church of Latter-Day Saints; another identified himself as a humanist-oriented Jewish ordained rabbi.

[7] It endeavored to encapsulate a layman's retrospective readings of an abbreviated historical spectrum within the pre-Civil War era of American Constitutional case law.

12. Their Own Worst Enemies

One of the oldest, most obvious and least original antisemitic tropes was voiced by Amb. White when he lunched with Lord Rothschild in London. A topic of their conversation was the treatment of Jews in Russia (White, 1905b). Speaking in his autobiographical tome as an *emeritus* authority about international diplomacy, he cited "apparently trustworthy sources" to the effect that the Rothschild bank had, in part, financed reparations fomented after the Russo-Japanese War: "I can think of nothing so sure to strengthen the anti-Semites throughout the world" (p. 4).[1]

On an earlier occasion, Amb. White regurgitated similar third-hand hearsay that he attributed to an American Consul in Germany:
"He had taken an American lady on a business errand to the bank of Baron Rothschild, and, after their business was over, presented her to the great banker. It happened that a Confederate loan had been financed in Europe by a Baron Erlanger, also a Frankfurt financial magnate, and by birth a Hebrew. In the conversation that ensued between the lady and Baron Rothschild, the latter said: 'Madam, my sympathies are entirely with your country; but is it not disheartening to think that there are men in Europe who are lending their money and trying to induce others to lend it for the strengthening of human slavery? Madam, *none but a converted Jew would do that*'" [emphasis in original text] *(ibid.,* p. 96).

In an earlier self-revelatory fragment, he wrote:
"One little outgrowth of my religious intolerance was quickly nipped in the bud. As I was returning home one evening with a group of scampish boys, one of them pointed out the "Jew store"— in those days a new thing [in Syracuse]—and reminded us that the proprietor worshiped on Saturday and, doubtless, committed other abominations. At this, with one accord, we did what we could to mete out Old Testament punishment for blasphemy—we threw stones at his door. My father, hearing of this, dealt with me sharply and shortly, and taught me most effectually to leave dealing with the Jewish religion to the Almighty. I have never been tempted to join in any anti-Semitic movement whatever"[2] *(ibid.,* p. 518).

"Puerile antigens" presumably immunized Amb. White against personal susceptibility to deplorable prejudices. Regrettably, such maladies reman rife within American history. The "past is prologue" cliché informs us that simmering historical animosities likely linger beyond succeeding generations. Beneath the rhetoric of the Pres. White/Prof. Adler feud, the respective postgraduate educations of both men in America and abroad paralleled one other. They shared a mutual disdain for hierarchical religiosity.

In his preface to *The Diaries of Andrew D. White,* editor Ogden observed that they [the diaries] were "never introspective, and, excepting a few emotional outbursts, what he writes is never very revealing about his state of mind..." (p. vii). Amb. White, in his autobiography published a half-century earlier, cited accusations during his earlier life about what others had characterized as "my indifferentism" (White, 1905b, p. 562). A few pages onward, he named "Rabbis Weinstock and Jacobs" *(ibid,* p. 573) together with four more clerics amongst his fervent supporters. They had ostensibly opined against the evils of fanatacism in America. Judging from phraseology cited in the table of contents of Amb. White's autobiography, adroit readers must still fend for themselves in construing his précis about the "sobering effects upon me of 'spiritualistic' fanaticism" *(ibid.,* p. xix). One may peripherally wonder what motivated Amb. White to attend Felix's Sunday morning lectures in Manhattan on Jan. 5, 1890 (Ogden, p. 295), May 10, 1891 *(ibid.,* p. 309) and Dec. 19, 1909 *(ibid.,* p. 425). In retrospect, such excursions seem to smack of an almost patronizing self-indulgence. Their face-to-face contact was documented upon at least one such occasion.

Historians with the halls of academia have often proven reluctant to overcome their intellectual taboos in coping with purported Judeo-centric patterns of behavior. Aside from the subconscious barriers Pres./Amb. White apparently attributed to himself, his retrospective fixations about "predatory Hebrews" [quotation marks in text] *(ibid.,* p. 171), or the ingrained "counterfeiting" tendencies of American-naturalized Russian Jews *(ibid.,* p. 105) speak for themselves. Further aspects of his diplomatic perspectives on U.S. State Department regulations were likely reflective of past roles he may have exercised in gauging international "evils" *(ibid.,* p. 172).

Judging from his late adult writings, Amb. White (1905b) thought that the fate of Jews ultimately depended on decisions made by them to change their own ways. While acknowledging "the murderous cruelties against the Jews of Kishineff," he was strident in extolling the "fact that Russia sets a high value upon its citizenship." According to his rationale:

"Its value, whatever it may be, is the result of centuries of struggles, of long outpourings of blood and treasure and Russians believe that it has been bought at too great a price and is in every way too precious to be lavished and hawked about as a thing of no value.[3] On the other hand, when one sees how the citizenship in the United States which ought to have been a millionfold more precious than that of Russia, is conferred loosely upon tens of thousands of men absolutely unfit to exercise it—whose exercise of it seems, at times, likely to destroy republican government" *(ibid.,* p. 39).

White's rhetorical hesitancy in tackling imperial Russia's history of pogroms against its Jewish minorities is problematic. His equivocations speak for themselves:

"There are more Israelites in Russia than in all of the remainder of the world; and they are crowded together, under most exasperating regulations, in a narrow district just inside her western frontier, mainly extending through what was formerly Poland, with the result that fanaticism—Christian on one side and Jewish on the other—has developed enormously. The Talmudic Rabbis are there at their worst; and the consequences are evil, not only for Russia, but for our own country. *The immigration which comes to us from these regions is among the very worst that we receive from any part of the world. It is, in fact an immigration of the unfittest* [emphasis added]; and although noble efforts have been made by patriotic Israelites in the United States to meet the difficulty, the results have been far from satisfactory" (pp. 51-52).

Amb. White had long been a resolute opponent of slavery and an outspoken proponent of citizenship for the Negro. As a philanthropist, he allied himself with individuals of wealth. While anticipating a $300,000 bequest from his deceased father's estate, he formulated a bold attempt to curry favor with the abolitionist Gerrit Smith[4] in an unsuccessful attempt to promote his specific vision of an "ideal university" (White, 1862). He subsequently succeeded in partnering with Ezra Cornell, who donated $400,000 toward an endowment for this goal. Another prospective donor whom White courted was Joseph Seligman (White, 1874b). The basis for such belief is predicated upon archival correspondence referenced in another letter he (White, 1874a) authored to an unknown addressee on Mar. 10, 1874 citing self-aggrandizing testimony he gave on Dec. 19, 1873 at a legislative hearing in Albany that soon thereafter appeared in print.

During his post-Cornell tenure, Amb. White helped coordinate the activities of the Russian Famine Relief Committee of the United States. He and others prevailed on Andrew Carnegie in supporting global harmony while fostering establishment of the International Peace Palace at the Hague in Holland.

The plaintiff plea articulated in Fig. 3 remains as an enduring testimonial of Prof.Adler's disdain for Pres. White's lurching moral compass about church/state neutrality that continued to vacillate "Far Above Cayuga's Waters."

---

[1] At first glance, former Amb. White's autobiographical snippet seems like a playful aside in which he seems to be poking fun at himself while sharing blame for a youthful prank. Upon further reflection, the thrust of his 'quasi-confession' looks evocative of the Shakespearean adage: "Thou doth protest too much!" It attempts to equate the juvenile defacement of a Jewish merchant's business premises— either consciously or unconsciously—with an 'absolution' in perpetuity for a storekeeper's purported commercial sins upon a biblical Sabbath. In like manner, autobiographer White's predilections toward nurturing antisemitic tropes about spiraling banking conspiracies by international Jewry recur too frequently for happenstance.

[2] Charles Dickens popularized the term "telescopic philanthropy." A noted cultural historian has characterized such phraseology as "the kind of benevolence that, tinged by racism and classism, works best from a safe distance" (Fry, 2020, p. 74). An array of Pres./Amb. White's historical stances seemingly reflected similar attitudes.

[3] Amb. White's pronouncements about the gravitas of Russian *vis-à-vis* American citizenship seem significant. They were voiced after he concluded his two-year stint as a foreign ambassador in St. Petersburg. Comments from his personal diary on Apr. 22, 1855, as a 23-year old volunteer/aide at the U.S. Embassy while a French translator (the *lingua franca* for European diplomacy) some 37 years earlier, also seems significant. Then—perhaps inspired by life in Tsarist Russia (Varoli, 2020), he came to inspect the prestigious Cadet Corps, visiting the dorms and classrooms and remarking: "We commenced our tour about the immense institution in which are educated boys of all ages for the Army" *(ibid.,* p. 2, and White, 1855, pp. 65-66, diary entry for Apr. 22, 1855). Ostensibly reflected in that initial six-month stay in St. Petersburg, starting in late October in 1854, was his fascination with feudal-era vestiges of pre-adolescent servitude. Unlike others of his generation familiar with training at academies like West Point, exposure to such military activities was not a part of the young White's collegiate education. At less than 5 feet 5 inches in height, he had always been sensitive about his physical stature. The fate of Russo-Jewish conscriptees was, by contrast, was far less assuring. All Jewish males at age 12, pursuant to the 1825 decree of Tsar

Nicholas, were subjected to indefinite periods of military service, relegated to second-class citizenship and forbidden from ever becoming officers.

[4] He was a Madison County resident who led the so-called "Secret Six." This committee of wealthy abolitionists including Samuel Gridley Howe, Franklin Benjamin Sanborn, George L. Stearns, Thomas Wentworth Higginson and Theodore Parker had also backed the exploits of John Brown in Kansas.

13. Of Jewish Culture and Ethical Culture

Idealizing a personal belief system predicated on a philosophy of rhetorical fairness and humanitarianism may embellish an aura of wholesomeness. A nebulous vagueness about the existence or nonexistence of a deity may also have tended to vaporize the innate human truths he sought to broaden. The issue of wealth distribution seems to conflict with his concept of moral idealism. To the extent that the progressive thrust of the Ethical Culture Society's *avant-garde* movement continued to thrive, some advocates were left wondering if Jewish identity in America was itself at stake.

For the senior Marshall, the survival of Jewish culture itself had always been a pivotal global issue. The spoken tongues/dialects, head coverings (if any), political disparities or even the tenuous existence or nonexistence of a personal God were eclipsed by the continuous atrocities of antisemitic pogroms in eastern Europe. Once restricted socioeconomic opportunities became more accessible to semi-religious Jews, many were lulled into an inertia of faith in their appetite for systematized religiosity. Marshall, long prior to the state of Israel's birth, ultimately came to rebalance aspiring Zionist/anti-Zionist or socialistic Arbeiter Bund "-isms" *vis-à-vis* the greater expedient of Jewish existence in an ominous world.

As the 20th century progressed, the Adirondack Mountains became a multiseasonal destination for prosperous Jewish vacationers seeking fresh-air escapes from metropolitan congestion. Accessibility via rail, auto and air travel became easier and antisemitic slurs less noticeable. Hopefully, all of mankind will continue to cherish the legacies of the Adler/Marshall trailblazers together with the humanitarian, naturalist and conservation movements they helped foster.

14. "Rip Van Winkle-esque" Reawakenings and Righting Wrongs

Focusing upon the final year of Pres. White's administration at Cornell University, he was departing upon a southern sojourn when the contents of Fig. 1 landed upon his desk.[1] An anonymous journalist had presumably been privy to an issue of his hometown newspaper, the *Syracuse Standard,* that alluded to a sensitive issue *(i.e.,* "Is Cornell?" paraphrasing co-founder White, "Christian, but not sectarian"). A secretary in Ithaca dispatched the data in question to W. C. Russel who was on a family visit in downstate Newburgh, N.Y. while serving as acting Vice President.

A reader of the undated missive may note that it begins with an innuendo about "infidel colleges." Fig. 2 includes an editorial rejoinder published in the *Cornell Daily Sun.* It was undoubtedly reviewed by Editor-in-Chief S. M. Stevens. The text heralded the proclamation that "Cornell prides itself upon being a nonsectarian institution; but never has and, it never will, pose as an exponent of atheism." Readers reviewing Fig. I are then left with scant choice in differentiating between a familial name such as "Rev. George R. Vandewater[2] or others like "Gluck and Frankenheimer."[3] They may merely speculate which of the last duo appears to "pose as an exponent of atheism."

The full text of W. C. Russel's letter of April 30, 1885 to Pres. White seems salient. He wrote in part, "I could not under any circumstances believe" such journalistic 'canards.' I sent your letter to Adler as you requested and I enclose his answer to my note…Adler's logic is unanswerable and at his point of view, his feelings very intelligible. Were I a Jew or Mohammedan, I should sympathize with him."

The dismissal of Felix a decade earlier by Pres. White was then and there revivified. The interim church/state vacillations had not abated. Trustee/ benefactor Henry W. Sage[4]—believing that Cornell University needed a dedicated building for religious services—funded such a family-named chapel. Unlike other contemporary institutions of higher learning, it had always eschewed student-chapel attendance.[5] The following year, the Sage family endowed the construction of separate housing for female students.

Many came to consider Trustee Sage a third co-founder of Cornell University.

It is unlikely that Felix would have been invited to attend a Cornell University sponsored reception at Morelli's Restaurant in Manhattan on the evening of April 29, 1885. It was led by Pres. White and attended by humorist Mark Twain was a guest speaker. Among the festivities was a celebration of the election victory of Trustee/Rev. Vandewater over opposing candidate/alumnus Frankenheimer. We may recall that the vanquished aspirant Frankenheimer had been chided in an issue of the *Cornell Daily Sun* as "an advanced pupil of Felix Adler" who supposedly relished "an inherited dislike of Christianity (Fig. I).

Pursuant to the imprimatur creating the scholarly chair endowed by Trustee/benefactor Sage:

"I desire to put on the record for permanent remembrance this statement: 'That my chief object in founding this professorship is to secure for Cornell University for all coming time the services of a teacher who shall instruct students in mental philosophy and ethics from a definitely Christian standpoint'" (Bishop, pp. 247-248).

According to the same historian, "proper work in philosophy was not undertaken until Dr. Jacob Gould Schurman arrived in 1886" *(ibid.,* p. 167).

At the beginning of the following academic year, prior to the inauguration of Charles Kendall Adams as the second president of Cornell University on Nov. 19, 1885, the Board of Trustees, with H. W. Sage's enthusiastic endorsement, designated Prof. Jacob Gould Schurman as "Chair of Christian Ethics and Mental Philosophy."

On Nov. 11, 1892, Prof. Schurman was installed as the third president of Cornell University. The clerical benediction recited by Rev. C. M. Taylor (1891) at the culmination of his ascension to the position was pointedly Christian: "Now, may the blessings of God, the Father Almighty, the grace of our Lord and Savior Jesus Christ, and the fellowship and communion of the Holy Ghost, abide with us forever, Amen" (p. 81).

Evolving events often overtake dark historical periods. Pres. Schurman was speaking out, advocating for "Jewish preachers…and Trustees" *(ibid.,* p. 71). Early in 1896, Rabbi E. G. Hirsch delivered the first Jewish clerical address at Sage Chapel. In 2014, The Schwerner-Cheney-Goodman Memorial installed a stained-glass window in Sage Chapel eulogizing the lives of three murdered civil rights workers (Michael Schwerner, '61, James Cheney and Andrew Goodman). Goodman's parents, also Cornell University alumni, were Carolyn Druckman Goodman, '35; Robert Goodman, '35 and '36).

Upon the death of Felix Adler in 1933, Oswald Garrison Villard, Sr., editor of The Nation and founding member of NAACP, memorializing his memory of him in a regular column ("Issues and Men"), wrote: "The Passing of a Great American Jew" (vol. 137, p. 473).

Amb. White dispatched a cable from St. Petersburg on May 18, 1893 to the U.S. State Department. He invoked phraseology about Russian history that for him may have seemed commonplace. "Jew baiting," in his parlance, meant that "For some time past...the old edicts against them [Jews] have been enforced in various parts of the Empire with more and more severity." In ensuing passages, he contrasted "millionaire Jews... who have amassed so much wealth" in other parts of the world with "Israelites of the humbler class [who] find it more and more difficult to reenter Russia..." One's imagination is in flux while attempting to compare portrayals of "Jew baiting" mentioned in his cable from imperial Russia with his autobiographical screed about "immigration of the unfittest" to America some dozen years later (White, 1905b, pp. 51-52).

In January of 1911, Marshall delivered a speech entitled "Russia and American Passports" at a national meeting of the Union of American Hebrew Congregations. In it, he admonished his audience was "not to rate trade volume over dignity, the dollar over men." It is unlikely that Prof. Adler had been an invitee.

Jewish travelers in Russo-Slavic Europe were known to have been imperiled by foreign edicts restricting movements of citizens far more onerous than they found tolerable. Euphemistic terminology such as "border-naturalization-extortion" was coined by some victims. Paramount among the causes, constitutional lawyer Louis Marshall had always championed was the ending of restrictions against immigration to America (see Chapter 6). Ultimately, Marshall was unsuccessful in his campaign to lift restrictions stalemating the opening of emigration to the United States from the Pale of Jewish Settlement.

It was unlikely that Marshall would have brooded over his frustrated efforts as an erstwhile advocate for immigration reforms even if he had attended Amb. White's aforementioned "semi-humanitarian" speech on Dec. 6, 1911 in New York City. He more likely may have reminisced about his

54

own leadership roles in arresting Cornell University's exclusive institutional dominion in administering the so called "land-grant" funds in New York State that originated under the aegis of ex-Pres. White. Questionable late 19th-century practices in managing Adirondack acreage dedicated for a demonstration forest preserve led to the Legislature's defunding of the endeavor.[6] Such an end result paved the way for Marshall enable Syracuse University to supersede Cornell University as a rival "land-grant" institution for the promotion of professional forestry.

In Chapter 37 of the *Autobiography of Andrew D. White* subtitled "Walks and Talks with Tolstoy," the author's dialogue with his subject took place during March of 1894. In a colloquy about lynching in the American South, White cited "Goldwin Smith's profound remark that some lynchings are proofs not so much of lawlessness than a respect for law (White, 1905b, p. 77). The ensuing text, appearing several paragraphs later,[7] is remarkable:

"On my attempt to draw from him [Tolstoy] some statement as to what part of American literature pleased him most, he said that he had read some publications of the New York and Brooklyn Society of Ethical Culture and that he knew and liked the writings of Felix Adler" *(ibid.,* pp. 82-83).

In an ancillary context, we may question why Amb. White chose to amass a premier treasure trove about American Mormonism. Earlier, he had scorned such movements that he had viewed as deviant cults[8]. In his words, Tolstoy came to characterize Mormonism as follows:

"He thought that two-thirds of their religion deception; but, said on the whole he preferred a religion which professed to have dug its sacred books out of the earth to one that pretended that they were let down from heaven" (p. 87).

Upon the evening of April 11, 1906, Mark Twain was a keynote speaker at a literary gathering in New York City to fete Maxim Gorki (a/k/a Alexei Maximovitch Peskov). The reputation of the latter honoree became so controversial after April 14, 1906 that he and his entourage were denied hotel lodging. Local press reports had branded him an adulterer and accessory to a bombing murder after having expressed sympathy for two accused miners.

Husband and wife John and Prestonia (née Mann) Martin—a utopian-minded couple of American/Fabian Socialist inclinations—offered the second floor of their home on Staten Island as an immediate refuge for the *persona non grata* Gorki group. The Martin family thereupon hosted the Russian entourage at their home on Staten Island. Such guests included author Maxim Gorki, common-law companion Madame Maria Andreeva, Nikolai Evgen'evich Burenin, his secretary and Zalman Sverdlov, Gorki's Jewish-raised adopted son (a/k/a Zinovy Peshkov), who had already been living in Manhattan (Rayner-Canham, 1992, pp. 54-55).

The erstwhile American envoy to Russia (A. D. White, 1906) and Felix Adler were apparently upon the same page in their outspoken campaigns to slur the group led by Gorki.

According to the unpublished notes of host John Martin (Holtsman, 1962):
"At the time I was a member of the Board of Trustees for the Society of Ethical Culture in New York City of which Dr. Felix Adler... was executive leader. He came to my house somewhat unexpectedly one Sunday when a number of the Russian colony from Manhattan and Brooklyn were present. I learned later that members of the Ethical Culture Society had complained that I was harboring a wicked, dissolute man and his paramour, and Dr. Adler had come specifically to ascertain the facts. He took away with him a copy of a letter I had written to the local paper and which he used to appease the complainants" (pp. 231 & 234, footnote 16).

If true, the foregoing account tends to cast an ominous unsavoriness upon the *persona* of Dr. Adler.

The Martin couple's Adirondack estate, Summer Brook, sat astride Hurricane Ridge near the Glenmore Institute at Keene, N.Y. The Canadian nuclear physicist, Harriet Brooks[9] (who had been an academician at Barnard College in New York City where she became acquainted with the aforecited "cast of characters") joined them after traveling by train from Montreal to Westport, N.Y. Their group was housed upon the grounds of the estate's in a lodge named Arisponet (an anagrammatization of "Prestonia"). The possible existence of a romantic relationship involving Harriet at the Arisponet cabin during the Summer and early Fall of 1906 remains conjectural (Raynor-Canham, pp. 65 & 143, fn. 3).

One surmises that Felix Adler soon gleaned first-hand knowledge of the Gorki entourage's activities in the Adirondacks near Keene, N.Y. Over the summer of 1906, both resided in neighboring homesteads. Arisponet, long venerated by Russian *literati*, is where Gorky penned his classic Russian novel *(The Mother)* about revolutionary conversion and struggle.

---

[1] Felix Adler may have likewise been aware of the Apr. 10, 1885 announcement in the *Cornell Daily Sun* that Pres. White "…had gone South for the benefit of his health. His lecture in Modern History will be read by Mr. Huffcut."

[2] The "Van" prefix in a family name such as "Vandewater" (*i.e.,* 'Rev. George R.') may understandably have suggested a heritage fostered by a sect like the Dutch Reform faith in the colonial era of New York City.

[3] Judging from the phraseology upon the face of Fig. 3, names like Gluck and Frankenheimer were clearly foremost in Felix Alder's thinking when he implored W. C. Russel: "…are not we radicals, citizens of the State and entitled to the same rights and considerations as our Christian friends?" Notwithstanding Frankenheimer's initial failure as a trustee candidate, Pres. White came to include him as "one of seven Jews" in his personal tally singling out the religiosity of fraternity members at Cornell University. Soon after, *via* a letter Frankenheimer wrote on July 8, 1885, he explicitly denied ever having been exposed to any religious intolerance under the aegis of Pres. White's tutelage while an undergraduate at his *alma mater*.

[4] He professed "not to care anything about the professors' opinions but…was always in a fever lest somebody should think of him as an infidel…Sage was happy…that the Board was finally 'waking up to the knowledge that they hire the professors who are irreligious and who advertise this fact abroad'…" (Keller, p. 57).

[5] On November 11, 1892, the Board of Trustees—then chaired by Henry W. Sage—designated J. G. Schurman as Cornell University's third president. In his inaugural oration, he asserted *inter alia*: "It would be shameful, were it not tragic proof of our poverty, that Cornell University is still without chairs of Semitic and Oriental Civilization, even without a professorship of that Hebrew literature which has furnished the sublimest content of modern civilization" (Schurman, p. 74). The purity of Board Chairman Sage's *credo* coupled with his institution's newly installed chief executive were to undergo further testing.

[6] The extent, if any, to which assorted Ithaca-based "timber barons" may have also been blameworthy remains unclear.

[7] Count Tolstoy was atheist Prof. Vladimir V. Nabokov's favorite Russian author. For more than a decade, he, his wife Véra (*née*) Slonim and their son Dimitri were home-renters in Ithaca, N.Y. Room 238 at "Goldwin Smith Hall" had doubled as their "academic address" while they were free to roam elsewhere. Outside his office, a statue of Pres. White, in scholarly robes, is today seated as an impressive sentinel before the building's entrance. It is tempting to wonder what he may have thought about the philosophical *gravitas* of such hosts as had "symbolically" sheltered him.

[8] A quarter-century beforehand, the 37-year-old Prof. White was afforded a first-

hand opportunity to examine the "disinterred" Cardiff Giant. After an initial period of indecision, he was not so gullible as to conclude that what turned into a "carnival hoax" had been scientifically plausible.

[9] Harriet *(née* Brooks) Pitcher (1876-1933) became the wife of Frank H. Pitcher. After two and a half decades of their married life, she predeceased him. He had risen to the position of Chief Engineer of a municipal utility concern in Montreal. Neither he nor his wife were destined to reenter the academic world. The couple had three children, only one of whom (Paul Brooks Pitcher) outlived them. The surviving lad contracted tuberculosis in 1931 and required "a year 'curing' at Saranac Lake, N.Y." (Rayner-Canham, *ibid.,* p. 98). Due to her own failing health, Harriet may been afforded limited occasions upon which to visit him in the Adirondack Mountains. Fifteen years beforehand, as a thirtyish single woman exiting from academia with graduate fellowships from Bryn Mawr College and abroad, she summered over a couple of months in the same chain of mountains. Let us digress to note the circumstances leading to her untimely death some two and a half decades afterwards. It may have been hastened by her work with radium. Encompassing most of the third decade of her life, she had collaborated in nuclear research with future Nobel laureates Ernest Rutherford in Canada and England as well as Madame Marie Curie in Paris. It is this 15-month period in her life—beginning with the arrival of Maxim Gorki and his followers in New York City on April 10, 1906 and her London wedding day on July 13, 1907— that is the focus of this supplemental endnote. During this time, she became a significant figure amongst Gorki supporters. She terminated a planned marriage to Bergen Davis, a Columbia University physicist (Rayner-Canham, *ibid.,* p. 45). She submitted her resignation to Barnard College *(ibid.,* p. 50). She became reacquainted with her future husband, who had been her graduate demonstrator/ lecturer in physics while she was an undergraduate student at McGill University. She mainly mingled with Fabian socialists, Russian intelligentsia and Bolshevik revolutionaries in Adirondacks.

15. A Personal Coda

At the outset of researching data for this booklet, the transgenerational families of Felix Adler and Louis Marshall were the main two clans within my retrospective lines of sight. Such focuses subsequently widened to include linkages with the *personae*[1] of Andrew Dickson White, his nephew Ernest Ingersoll White and other of their immediate kin (including a New York State Governor). Ezra Cornell[2] preceded them. Like myself as the last-in-line pedestrian who had once ambled along Salina Street in Syracuse, all of us were central New Yorkers. The city's classically Greco-Roman name had reputedly been expropriated from a gazette in the hip-pocket of a Revolutionary War surveyor. "The Salt City" soon became the future metropolis's nickname.

It became the destination—just prior to the economic crash of 1929—at which my émigré parents and three older siblings finally reunited as a family in America when all managed to exit from what had been known as the Pale of Jewish Settlement. My father and eldest brother (then a twelve-year-old lad) led the five-member family's exodus. My mother with two younger offspring (a daughter and baby boy) were left behind in Russia for almost six years. Two more sons were thereafter born to our parents on this side of the Atlantic Ocean. I am the junior of them.

Unlike our parents and my three oldest siblings, I had neither known hunger nor been exposed to massacres of Jews in Russo-Slavic pogroms. So too, had I been spared the after-effects of international conflicts such as those occasioned by the Russo-Japanese War and World War I.

In Syracuse, the five senior members of the Ginsburg family resided in habitable circumstances and became naturalized U.S. citizens. Although I had been enthralled with Tom Mix movies as a youngster, our mother often dragged me to Russian films. She also relished reading works of such Russian authors as Mikhail Lermontov, whose English translations subsequently became familiar to me.

I was stationed in then West Germany over a two-year period as a newly minted lawyer serving in the U.S. armed forces (as had two of my older brothers, the eldest of whom was a World War II era veteran). Among the most vivid memories of my post-World War II military service were visits to former extermination camps and a mass cemetery situated in what was then East Berlin with statuary depicting Mother Russia mourning her dead.

Dr. Felix Adler became known to me as an idiosyncratic (my adjective) philosopher I initially associated with the Adirondack Mountains. Not until adulthood had I begun to think of him as a contemporary of Louis Marshall and proponent of the Ethical Culture movement. Not until embarking upon this historical retrospective did I realize that the White family often frequented Saratoga Springs in the Adirondacks over much of the third quarter of the nineteenth century.

Pres. White presumably adulated the intellectual pedigree of Prof. Goldwin Smith when he recruited him to join the faculty of the fledging institution that he helped co-found in 1865. Both in North America and abroad, an unexpurgated litany of self-professed racist epithets and strident antisemitic rants streamed from the latter academician's pen. It remains a grim reality that—in the annals of scholarly thought—Goldwin Smith's historical heritage has eluded commensurate opprobrium for his unapologetic behavior. The indulgence that Pres. White evinced to curry the quintessential Englishman's favor within their clique of intimate confidants in Ithaca was, and still, remains odious to me. Until recently, it has been disquieting that Cornell University has proven prone to perpetuating such institutional shame by desisting from altering the name of a principal campus building still sanctifying the life of Prof. Goldwin Smith.[3]

The *Autobiography of Andrew D. White,* the author's *magnum opus,* was initially published in 1905. Not until 1951were 65 handwritten volumes of personal diaries discovered. They were bereft of any entries between July 6, 1856 and January 2, 1865.[4]

Less discernable to me are the root causes of Pres. White's self-inflicted wounds to his reputation. To what extent, if any, will his historical standing remain unblemished from an incontrovertible nexus with Prof. Goldwin Smith? Over several decades, there has been a *sub rosa* realization in Ithaca that the latter figure was a renowned racial bigot.[5]

Among the perversely prejudiced attitudes that Prof. Goldwin Smith shared with Pres. White were their tiresome slogans about Jewish international banking cabals. In the educational traditions that have enlightened me, I was taught that responses to questionable historical theses inevitably merit further scrutiny; it is only by looking at commonalities and differences that we may learn. Comparing or grading human suffering and historical trends in moral breakdown is beyond my know-how. Nevertheless, I find it particularly grievous that over most of the 20th century—both before and after publication of Pres. White's autobiography—a "quasi-okaying" and/ or exorcising of blighted historicism has been countenanced. Recent headway in Ithaca has seemingly begun to surge in a more favorable direction.

On March 3, 2009, an article appeared in the *Cornell Alumni Magazine* entitled "Goldwin Smith: Anti-Semite?" It was co-authored by two Cornell University faculty historians (Altschuler and Isaac Kramnick, p. 38). Fast-forward a further dozen years to December 15, 2020, when a column printed in the *Cornell Daily Sun* was headlined: "Trustees Vote to Remove Goldwin Smith, Who Held Racist, Sexist Beliefs, From Honorary Professor Titles" (Giafurta and Greene, p. 1).

To what extent, if any, have the unsavory aspects of Goldwin Smith's historical behavior—albeit by extension—continue to tarnish the character of a co-founder of Cornell University? May the Board of Trustees vote to ameliorate ensuing damages long tolerated as part of its institutional heritage? Or shall they merely choose to remain dismissive of posterity as if history has been frozen in a time warp so as to cloister aspects of a pioneering-educator's *alter ego?*

---

[1] I am an alumnus of Cornell University and the Syracuse University College of Law. Pres. Joseph R. Biden, Jr., '68 and his son (Hon. Joseph R. "Beau" Biden, III, '94), a deceased Delaware State Attorney General, are also among the latter institution's *alumni.* Putting my matriculation in historical context, Paul Shipman Andrews was then concluding his tenure as Dean; his grandfather was Hon. Charles Andrews, who had been a life-long confidant and personal lawyer for Amb. White. As a jurist, Louis Marshall had served as Chief Judge of the New York State Court of Appeals, and had often stood before him as an appellate litigator.

[2] He detested Syracuse as a den of sin, citing instances where he was twice robbed of wages he earned as a young man. Overcoming White's preference for Syracuse instead of Ithaca as the site for their University, Ezra Cornell reputedly gave $25,000 to induce other Syracusans to withdraw their legislative opposition to the creation of a rival university based in Ithaca. In the absence of evidentiary proof, perhaps such "consideration" was bottomed upon a reallocation of so-called "land script" in circulation under the Morrill Land-Grant Colleges Act.

[3] It may have originally been financed with some funds partly underwritten by the State of New York.

[4] A compendium published by an editor (Ogden, 1959) of such diaries asserted in his annotations that they were: "...not the story of a man who used...[them]... to record his innermost thoughts. On the contrary, he keeps these thoughts well concealed. But he was not an introspective person. He was not even a philosophical person. He was objective, and the world he was exploring was a factual world. Obviously fond of his friends, and lonely when they were not about him, he describes no intimacies. He loved the society of women, yet showed no disposition to fall in love. Even his relation to his sweetheart, Mary, at home is somewhat ambiguous. At least the thought of her did not seem to interfere with the purposes of his Wanderjahre"..." (pp. 141-142). On June 30, 1888, Ernest Ingersoll White (1870-1957), "a bright active college youth" departed on a European voyage with his mourning uncle, after the "dismaying death of his first wife" (Ogden, p. vi). This "favorite nephew...a young man of nineteen" *(ibid.)* and a "noble, lovely boy, God bless him always" *(ibid.,* p. 284, fn. 13). He graduated from Cornell University, completed his legal education at Columbia University and married Katharine Curtin Sage, a granddaughter of the aforesaid Henry W. Sage, whereupon the couple settled in Syracuse. He later financed the compilation of an edition of his deceased uncle's long missing diaries, the sole version of which appeared in print more than a half century after publication of the Autobiography of Andrew D. White (1905). Amongst such revivified diary entries, it became evident that Amb. White and/or son Frederick consulted psychiatrist S. Weir Mitchell, M.D. in Philadelphia on Apr. 17, 1888 (Ogden, p. 283) and Jan. 20, 1891 *(ibid.,* p. 306). On July 8, 1901 (per another entry), "my dear son took his own life with a rifle in his own house unable longer to bear the pain, distress and martyrdom which he had so long borne" *(ibid.,* p. 371). In the compiling editor's additional words about segments of such diary's entries: "They are not reflective...he was never given to the analysis of his own state of mind. The characterizations of the persons he met and knew are very fragmentary" *(ibid.,* p. vi).

[5] Biographers have written much about Pres./Amb. White's multi-faceted careers as educator, diplomat and philanthropic activist. His autobiographical narrative exceeds 1,200 pages, substantial segments of which center upon his personal role in mankind's history. It is apparent that an array of historian-academicians have—either wittingly or unwittingly—side-stepped salient features of his life. His activities as a 29½-year old citizen during America's Civil War, both here and abroad, present myriad questions. He was a descendent of wealthy bankers. Intra-personal relationships with immediate family members have proven difficult to document.

62

Appendix I: Illustrations

Fig. 1: An editorial note in April 10, 1885 issue of the *Cornell Sun*

We print on the first page of this issue an extract from the Syracuse *Standard* "A question for the Alumni." The question as to whom shall be chosen at commencement for our next alumni representative is one of much importance, considering the candidates who have already and will hereafter come up for the consideration of the alumni. The contests of the past two years for alumni trustee have created enough excitement, and the part which the trustee may play, be it beneficial or detrimental to the university, has been sufficiently well proven to impress upon the minds of all interested alumni the fact that it is quite essential for them to consider the policy and opinion of the candidates before deciding whom they shall support. Cornell prides herself upon being a non-sectarian institution; but never has and, it is hoped, never will, pose as an exponent of atheism. In the candidates mentioned for alumni trustee by the Syracuse *Standard* appear two men who represent opinions radically different; but the question whether a sectarian, educated in a non-sectarian institution, or one radically non-sectarian and educated in a non-sectarian institution is fitted to hold a position as trustee of this institution, representing the opinions of Cornell's alumni, is one which on thought it seems the alumni will not find it difficult to decide.

Transcript of Fig. 1:

We print on the first page of this issue an extract from the Syracuse Standard "A question for the Alumni." The question as to whom shall be chosen at commencement for our next alumni representative is one of so much importance, considering the candidates who have already and will hereafter come up for the consideration of the alumni. The contest of the past two years has created enough excitement, and the part which one trustee may play, be it beneficial or detrimental to the university, has been sufficiently well proven to impress upon the minds of all interested alumni the fact that it is quite essential for them to consider the policy and opinion of the candidates before deciding whom they shall support. Cornell prides itself upon being a non-sectarian institution; but never has and, it is hoped, never will, pose an exponent of atheism. In the candidates mentioned for alumni trustee by the Syracuse Standard appear two men who represent opinions radically different; but the question whether a sectarian, educated in a non-sectarian institution, or one radically non-sectarian and educated in a non-sectarian institution is fitted to hold a position as a trustee of this institution, representing the opinions of Cornell's alumni, is one which on thought it seems the alumni will not find it difficult to decide.

Fig. 2: "A Question for our Alumni" in the April 10, 1885 issue
of the *Cornell Sun*

ITHACA, N. Y., FRIDAY, APRIL 10, 1885

A Question for our Alumni.

Cornell Alumni have a singular opportunity to show whether the influence of that university is Christian or anti-Christian. Many good folks have tossed sleeplessly on their beds at night because some promising young friend was going to an "infidel" college. On the other hand, President White maintains that Cornell is Christian, but not sectarian. To the question whether a college can be Christian without allegiance to a creed, the alumni will vote "aye" or "no" next June when they elect one of their number to serve as a trustee of the university. Usually there are three or more candidates for the honor. This year only two have been nominated. Of these John Frankenheimer of New York is an advanced pupil of Felix Adler, and to a contempt for all religion adds an inherited dislike of Christianity. When Trustee Gluck, at last year's alumni meeting, presented a report of the university, in which he alluded to the fact that the Christian religion is being taught in Sage Chapel, Mr. Frankenheimer was on his feet at once, and vociferously demanded that so objectionable a clause be stricken out, incorporating in his speech a sneer at religion, at the management of a university which could teach exploded fallacies, and at a trustee who could praise such things. He was opposed in a warm debate which followed by the Rev. George R. Vandewater of Brooklyn, who meets Mr. Frankenheimer this year as a rival candidate for the trusteeship. Before he had been out of college ten years Mr. Vandewater had become rector of St. Luke's, the largest Episcopal church in Brooklyn, a position he now holds, had been mentioned for a Bishopric in the West, and had gained a fine reputation as an eloquent pulpit speaker and a successful Christian worker. There can be no doubt that Mr. Vandewater holds views exactly the opposite to Mr. Frankenheimer's, or that each well represents the extremists with whom he is classed. Assuming that each is personally beyond reproach, it seems to us that the coming election will show very well what attitude the alumni of Cornell hold toward Christianity.
— *Syracuse Standard.*

Transcript of Fig. 2:

A Question for our Alumni.

Cornell alumni have a singular opportunity to show whether the influence of that University is Christian or anti-Christian. Many good folks have tossed sleeplessly on their beds as night because some promising young friend was going to an "infidel" college. On the other hand, Pres. White maintains that Cornell is Christian, but not sectarian. To the question of whether a college can be Christian without allegiance to a creed, the alumni will vote "aye" or "no" next June when they elect one of their number to serve as trustee of the university. Usually there are three or more candidates for the honor. This year only two have been nominated. Of these, John Frankenheimer of New York is an advanced pupil of Felix Adler, and to a contempt for all religion adds an inherited dislike of Christianity. When Trustee Gluck, at last year's alumni meeting, presented a report of the university, in which he alluded to the fact that the Christian religion is being taught at Sage Chapel. Mr. Frankenheimer was on his feet at once, and vociferously demanded that so objectionable clause be stricken out, incorporating in his speech a sneer at religion, at the management of a university which could teach exploded fallacies, and at a trustee who could praise such things. He was opposed in a warm debate which followed by Rev. George R. Vandewater of Brooklyn, who meets Mr. Frankenheimer this year as rival candidate for the trusteeship. Before he had been out of college ten years, Mr. Vandewater had become rector of St. Luke's, the largest Episcopal church in Brooklyn, a position he now holds, had been mentioned for a bishopric in the West, and had gained a fine reputation as an eloquent pulpit speaker and a successful Christian worker. There can be no doubt that Mr. Vandewater holds views exactly the opposite to Mr. Frankenheimer's, or that each well represents the extremists with whom he is classed. Assuming that each is personally beyond reproach, it seems to us that the coming election will show very well what attitude the alumni of Cornell hold toward Christianity

Fig. 3: The April 22, 1885 letter of Felix Adler to W.C. Russel

Transcript of Fig. 3:

April 22, 1885

Dear Mr. Russel:

I am pained more than I can express by the course things are taking at Cornell University. The enclosed letter, which I herewith return with thanks, of course disposes of the personal allusions which were reported the New York "Sun." But I cannot help but regretting deeply the efforts of so distinguished a man as President White to establish the "Christian " character of his University. It seems to me that when he uses the word Christian he means thereby "moral in the best sense." But it is precisely this identification of the highest morality with so distinctively a that is peculiarly grating to the sensibilities of those who are not Christians and do not desire to be classed as such. After all, is not Cornell University our University? Is it not a State institution? And are not we radicals, citizens of the State and entitled to the same rights and to the same consideration as our Christian friends? With what feelings do you suppose that we read the utterances of the President of Cornell University in which he tries to establish that the tendency of his institution is in the direction of a Christian culture!

Appendix II:

A *Précis* of Composite Segments of *A Study of William Channing Russel as First Vice President and Acting President of Cornell University, 1870-1880* [1]

Dorothy Jean Keller (1961) wrote: "Andrew Dickson White, co-founder and President of Cornell University, was often absent from Ithaca, a situation necessitating the delegation of the Pres.'s administrative duties to another member of the University staff. White selected Russel for this role of administrative responsibility. The arrangement between the President and Russel continued until mid-1870 when White presented a plan for the purpose of formally establishing the office of Vice-President of the University. At White's request and with the approval of the Executive committee, Russel assumed office as Cornell University's first Vice-President on July 2, 1870. Six years later, White was granted a leave of absence from the University to serve as the United States minister to Germany; and on June 14, 1876, the Board of Trustees adopted a resolution vesting Russel 'with all of the powers and duties now belonging to the President'" (Keller, pp. 1-2).

* * *

Elaborating on Russel's tenure as Cornell University's first term as its acting president on Mar. 25, 1877, "the Adler issue had been a rather passive one [when] it was commencing to brew up to an impressive storm" (Keller, p. 34). Contrary to Kraut's assertion that Felix "left Cornell University of his own accord" (Kraut, p. 104). Keller wrote: "Russel feared the repercussions when and if the question of Adler's retention was presented before the Executive Committee. The Executive Committee would indubitably decline to renew the appointment, placing Adler in a position to allege that his failure to be reappointed by the University authorities was 'a new case of timidity in the face of the Church and the Press.' In an attempt to avoid this unpleasantness, Russel desired to let Adler leave on his own account at the conclusion of his lecture series. Joseph Seligman, who had endowed Adler's lectureship, was not willing to let the matter go. The situation became quite intense when, instead of allowing the professorship to lapse at the end of the year, Seligman offered to renew the endowment for a period of three years at no expense to the University, provided, of course, that the professorship would be given to Adler. Since the Trustees would not be meeting until June, Russel found himself confronted with a seemingly necessary but highly undesirable delay in respect to an official decision of Seligman's proposal. The interest and intense feelings which would be aroused when Adler's friends and the public learned that the Board of trustees, seated in full session, voted against Adler's reappointment portended, to Russel, ill for the University. The problem, however, was solved on May 3, 1877, when the Executive Committee passed on a resolution the purpose of which was to inform Seligman that the trustees of the university could not accept endowments for professorships only when they were given the power of selecting the professor. On this note, the whole affair lingered for a short while and then gave way to other and more pressing events" (p. 34).

* * *

Continuing with a passage pertaining to Keller's seminal thesis about Russel, Keller wrote: "Russel's anxiety to get Adler bundled off and away from Cornell without attracting excessive attention should not be construed, however, as a contradiction of his basic liberality in the area of religion. While Russel was impressed with the poor public relations Adler had created and could continue to create for the University, he felt an even greater concern in relation to the question of 'whether it is perfectly fair for us to knock away the foundations of those who base their religion on the Bible while we profess to be absorbed in secular education exclusively?' Aware of the many inconsistencies and misconceptions in the Bible and convinced that they should be pointed out, Russel nevertheless disputed the right of those claiming indifference to religion to do it. On this basis, then, Russel could support the University's plan for ridding itself of Adler, at the same time maintaining his own liberality in the expression of religious views" (p. 35).

---

[1] The decade-long parameter of author's dissertation is superfluous. Tenure of her subject as *de facto* Acting Pres. of Cornell was formalized by his Mar. 31, 1881 resignaton letter to the Executive Committee wherein he "promised to cease his connections... [as such]... at the semester's end." *Via* a formal Resolution that the full Board of Trustees promulgated while Pres. White as abroad, the said Prof. William Channing Russel, L.L.D. (1814-1896) had therefore been serving as its sole institutional vice president "with all of the powers and duties now belonging to the President."

Appendix III:

The Abridged Higher Education of Louis Marshall

Some 63 years have elapsed since the previously cited pair of LM/CR volumes appeared in print. Since then, another biography entitled *Louis Marshall and the Rise of Jewish Ethnicity in America* by M. M. Silver (2013) has been published. It in turn referenced *Louis Marshall: A Biographical Sketch* by Cyrus Adler who—in the quoted words of such memoirist—authored the "primary or sole account of Marshall's legal training" (pp. 11 and 543, fn. 36). Apart from Silver's tome, the ensuing essay encapsulates, in part, what your author has distilled from readily available archival data pertaining to Marshall's attitudes about legal education. Selectively excerpted are passages from the first of the above-cited set of volumes:

> **From Marshall to Israel Zangwill:** *"As to the biographical information that you desire, I may say that I'm entitled to the prefix 'The Honorable,' having been a member of three Constitutional Conventions of the state of New York, namely in 1890, 1894 and 1915...I have also been the recipient of the Honorary Degree of Doctor of Laws from Syracuse University and have recently been awarded the degree Doctor of Hebrew Laws by Hebrew Union College..."* [8/4/1920 letter @ pp. 1160-1161 (LM/CR)].

> **From Marshall to son Robert:** *"I expect to be in Syracuse on the 19th...and in the evening I am to deliver an address before the students of the Law School. It is remarkable how that institution has developed since we reorganized it about a year ago. We made a practically clean sweep of the faculty"* [8/4/20 letter @ p. 1144 (LM/CR)].

> **From Marshall to a "Country Lawyer:"** *"I know something about practicing in what is called the country, because from 1878 until 1894, I practiced in Syracuse. I either knew or was known by almost everybody not only in Syracuse, but also throughout Onondaga County and the adjoining counties..."* [2/27/1928 letter @ pp. 1144-1145 (LM/CR)].

> **From Marshall to Syracuse University College of Law Dean Paul Shipman Andrews:** *"For a variety, largely the pressure of*

duties, I have failed to answer your kind letter of Oct. 3, 1928, in which you called for permission to give my name to a law society about to be formed by members of the senior class of the Laws College of Syracuse University 'all of Jewish extraction. While under ordinary circumstances, I would consider it an honor to have my name associated with a Law Society, on mature reflection I feel constrained to decline it. To accept would impliedly approve what I regard to be a deplorable condition now prevailing in American colleges, namely, the exclusion of Jewish students, however exemplary morally and intellectually from college societies. Your letter discloses that this unfortunate condition now exists in the Law College, for you say 'there are already one or two societies in the law school to which these boys are not admitted. That can only be due to intellectual narrowness on the part of these societies, in every inconsistent with justice and fair play'... " [12/12/1928 letter @ pp. 272-273 (LM/CR)].

From Marshall to "A Discouraged Scholar:" *"When my father came to this country, unable to speak the language, friendless and alone, he worked on a farm. He worked as a track hand in railroad construction. He was a porter. He was a peddler. He tried his hand at a dozen different occupations. Yet he always rejoiced in his work and gained the respect of all who knew him. I never went to college for a single day. As a boy I did hard manual labor, which is now prohibited under the child Labor Laws, salted hides and calfskins, and did other work of a kind which to most people would be unattractive... "* [2/19/1929 letter @ pp. 1145-1147 (LMCR]).

From Marshall to Harold R. Medina, Standing Committee, Alumni Association, Columbia Law School: *"I really do not know whether I am considered an alumnus of the Law School of Columbia University or not. If I am, then it is very peculiar that it has not been until I have arrived at the mature age of seventy-two that I should receive a letter which is addressed to me as Dear Fellow Alumnus"* [3/9/1929 letter @ pp. 8-9 (LMCR)].

Bibliography

Adler, C. (2011). "Louis Marshall: A Biographical Sketch." *Louis Marshall: A Biographical Sketch and Memorial Addresses,* Cyrus Adler, Irving Lehman [and] Horace Stern, C. Adler & I. Lehman, eds. New York: The American Jewish Committee (pp. 21-55).

Adler, F. (1885). April 22nd letter to W[illiam] C[hanning] Russel at Cornell University Library Digital Collections (ADW_Papers_reel_046_page_400.jpg)

_____ (1892). *The Moral Instruction of Children.* New York: Appleton & Co.

_____ (1904). *The Negro Problem in the United States with Special Reference to Mr. Dubois' Book "The Souls o' Black Folks."* Philadelphia: S. Burns Weston.

_____ (1921). *The Revival of Anti-Semitism.* New York: The American Ethical Union.

Adler, H. (1891). *Hints for the Scientific Observation and Study of Children.* New York: The Teacher Co.

_____ (1939). Address given on Sept. 6th at the Keene Valley Historical Society entitled "Felix Adler, One of the Early Pioneers in Keene Valley at Beede's." A transcript is catalogued at the Keene Valley Archives (Keene Valley, N.Y.).

Altschuler, G. & Kramnick, I. (2009). "Goldwin Smith: Anti-Semite?—New Book Exposes Famed Author's Bias. *Cornell Alumni News*, vol. 111(5), p. 38.

"An Eminent Opinion: A Syracuse Attorney Earnestly Favors the Proposition. Louis Marshall, Syracuse." *Jewish Tidings*, May 2, 1890.

Anthony, T.V.W. (1928). May 17th letter to John H. Asperson. John S. Asperson Papers at the Schenectady Museum, Schenectady, N.Y.

Barnes, J. (1984). *Flaubert's Parrot.* New York: Knopf (p. 150).

Begley, L. (2009). *Why the Dreyfus Affair Matters.* New Haven, Conn.: Yale University Press.

Billikopf, D.M. (1973). *The Exercise of Judicial Power, 1789-1864.* New York: Vanguard Press.

Bishop, M. (1962). *A History of Cornell.* Ithaca, N.Y.: Cornell University Press.

Carson, R.M.L. (1927). *Peaks and People of the Adirondacks*. New York: Doubleday Publishers.

Comstock, A.B. (1952). *The Comstocks of Cornell: John Henry Comstock and Anna Botsford Comstock* (an autobiography by Anna Botsford Comstock). G.W. Herrick and R.G. Smith, eds. Ithaca, N.Y.: Comstock Publishing Associates.

Cornell, E. (1868). Feb. 3rd letter to Andrew Dickson White at Cornell University Library Digital Collections (Ithaca, N.Y.).

Cornell University Archives (1874). "Statistics of the Class of 1874." Cornell University Class of 1874 collection (#41-4-554).

Davis, D. (2009). "Goldwin Smith's Anti-Semitism Fuels Anger." *Cornell Daily Sun,* April 30th issue (https://cornellsun.com/2009/04/30/goldwin_smiths_anti_semitism_fuels_anger/).

"Errors of Socialism: Prof. Adler Gives Reasons for Calling it Impractical. INDIVIDUALITY IS CHECKED, HE SAYS. The Apathy of the Prosperous Toward the Poor, He Declares Has Caused Socialistic Creeds." *New York Times,* Jan. 28, 1895.

"Far Above Cayuga's Waters" (1870). Cornell University alma mater (traditional alumni song). Lyrics by A.C. Weeks and W.M. Smith.

"Felix Adler Papers MS #0011." Columbia University Archives, catalogued items "RUSSEL 220.01-16" and "WHITE, PRES-1."

Friess, H.L. (1944). "Introduction." *Felix Adler: Life and Destiny.* New York: American Ethical Union.

———— (1981). *Felix Adler and Ethical Culture: Memories and Studies,* L. Weingarten, ed. New York: Columbia University Press.

Fry, N. (2020). " 'The Undoing' is Empty Life-style Porn." *The New Yorker,* Nov. 16, 2020.

"George Marshall, 96, Pioneer in the Civil Rights Movement." *New York Times,* June 18, 2000.

Gifford, G.E., Jr. (1972). "Freud and the Porcupine." *Harvard Medical Alumni Bulletin,* vol. 4, pp. 28-31.

Ginsburg, L.M. (2001). *Israelites in Blue and Gray: Unchronicled Tales from Two Cities*. Lanham, Md.: University Press of America.

————— (2010). *Tales of and About Jewish Youth During the* Fin-de-Siécle *Era: An Annotated a Transitional Decade in Upstate New York.* Lanham, Md.: University Press of America.

_____ (2019). "The Dislodgment of Jews Within Eastern Europe Over Three Generations: A 'Ginsburg' Family's Resilience" (pp. 1-42 and p. 31), undated and unpublished manuscript archived at the Cornell University Library (Ithaca, N.Y.) under "Lawrence M. Ginsburg Family Publications" (1967-2012, cache #8410).

Glover, J.M. (1986). *A Wilderness Original: The Life of Bob Marshall.* Seattle: The Mountaineers.

Goldmark, J.C. (1930). *Pilgrims of '48: One Man's Part in the Austrian Revolution of 1848 and a Family Migration to America.* New Haven, Conn.: Yale University Press.

Goldmark, P., ed. (1914). *West Side Studies*, vol. 1-2. New York: Russell Sage Foundation.

Greenwald, R.A. (1998). "'More than a Strike:' Ethnicity, Labor Relations and the Origins of the Protocol of Peace in the New York City Ladies' Garment Industry." *Business and Economic History,* vol. 27(2), pp. 318-329.

Guttschen, R.S. (1974). *Felix Adler.* New York: Twain Publishers.

Handlin, O. (1957). "Introduction." *Louis Marshall: Champion of Liberty, Vol.I* C. Reznikoff, ed. Philadelphia: Jewish Publication Society of America (pp. ix-xli).

Hawkins, R.A. (2013). "The Marketing of Legal Services in the United States, 1855-1912: A Case Study of Guggenheimer, Untermyer & Marshall of New York City and Predecessor Partnerships." *American Journal of Legal History,* vol. 53(2): pp. 239-264.

Holtzman, F. (1962). "A Mission that Failed: Gor'kij in America." *The Slavic and East European Journal,* vol. 6(3): pp. 227-235.

Hopsicker, P. (2009). " 'Hebrews Not Allowed': How the 1932 Lake Placid Winter Olympic Games Survived the 'Restricted' Adirondack Culture, 1887-1932." *Journal of Sport History,* vol. 36(2), pp. 205-222.

"How Philadelphia Stands." *New York Times,* June 20, 1877.

Jewish Tidings (1890). May 2nd column titled "An Eminent Opinion: A Syracuse Attorney Earnestly Favors the Proposition. Louis Marshall, Syracuse."

Keller, D.J. (1961). "A Study of William Channing Russel as First Vice Pres. and Acting Pres. of Cornell University, 1870-1880." Unpublished dissertation for Master of Arts degree at Cornell University.

Kittlestrom, A. (2015). *The Religion of Democracy: Seven Liberals and the American Moral Tradition.* New York: Penguin Press.

Medoff, R. (2006). The Jews Should Keep Quiet: President Franklin D. Roosevelt, Rabbi Steven S. Wise and the Holocaust. *New York History,* vol. 98(3/4): pp. 397-421.

Kraut, B. (1979). *From Reform Judaism to Ethical Culture: The Religious Evolution of Felix Adler.* Cincinnati: Hebrew Union College Press.

Leonard, H.B. (1972). "Louis Marshall and Immigration Restrictions, 1906-1924." *American Jewish Archives,* vol. 24(1), pp. 6-26.

Lifshitz, E. (2010). "'Let Our Little People Go Free:' Felix Adler's Campaign for Social Justice in the Progressive Era." New York: unpublished senior thesis (Columbia University Department of History).

Marshall, L. (1890). May 2nd letter to editor of *The Jewish Tidings* titled "An Eminent Opinion: A Syracuse Attorney Earnestly Favors the Proposition" (p.1).

_____ (1908/1909). *Proceedings of the 5th National Conference of Jewish Charities.* Baltimore: Kohn & Pollock, Inc. (pp. 112-122).

_____ (1914). Nov. 26th address at dedication of the Jewish Social Institute Building in Syracuse reported in Nov. 27th issue of *The Syracuse Post-Standard* under headline: "HEBREWS OPEN INSTITUTE WITH MUCH CEREMONY—Dedication of New Building Epoch in Community—HALL FILLED TO CAPACITY."

_____ (1915). Dec. 30th petition as president of the American Jewish Committee to His Holiness Pope Benedict XV. *American Jewish Committee,* vol. 9, pp. 22-24.

_____ (1916). Jan. 17th letter to the editor of *The New York Times. Louis Marshall: Champion of Liberty* ("Selected Papers and Addresses"), C. Reznikoff, ed., vol. I. Philadelphia: The Jewish Publication Society of America (pp. 273-276).

_____ (1921). June 3rd letter to Isaac W. Frank. *Louis Marshall: Champion of Liberty* ("Selected Papers and Addresses"), C. Reznikoff, ed., vol. I. Philadelphia: The Jewish Publication Society of America (pp. 556-561).

_____ (1923). June 7th letter to Judah L. Magnes. *Louis Marshall: Champion of Liberty* ("Selected Papers and Addresses"), C. Reznikoff, ed., vol. II. Philadelphia: The Jewish Publication Society of America (pp. 911-913).

_____ (1924). Oct. 18th letter to S. W. Straus. *Louis Marshall: Champion of Liberty* ("Selected Papers and Addresses"), C. Reznikoff, ed., vol. II. Philadelphia: The Jewish Publication Society of America (pp. 883-888).

_____ (1926a). April 10th letter to Senator David A. Reed. *Louis Marshall:*

Champion of Liberty ("Selected Papers and Addresses"), C. Reznikoff, ed., vol. I. Philadelphia: The Jewish Publication Society of America (pp. 228-234).

_____ (1926b). April 14th letter to Senator David A. Reed. *Louis Marshall: Champion of Liberty, Liberty* ("Selected Papers and Addresses"), C. Reznikoff, ed., vol. I. Philadelphia: The Jewish Publication Society of America (pp. 235-236).

_____ (1928a). February 27th letter to "A Discouraged Scholar." *Louis Marshall: Champion of Liberty* ("Selected Papers and Addresses"), vol. II. C. Reznikoff, ed. Philadelphia: Jewish Publication Society of America (p. 869).

_____ (1928b). May 5th letter to Robert Marshall. *Louis Marshall: Champion of Liberty* ("Selected Papers and Addresses"), C. Reznikoff, ed., vol. II. Philadelphia: The Jewish Publication Society of America (pp. 1169-1173).

_____ (1928c). Dec. 12th letter to Dean Paul Shipman Andrews. *Louis Marshall: Champion of Liberty* ("Selected Papers and Addresses"), C. Reznikoff, ed., vol. I, ed. Philadelphia: The Jewish Publication Society of America (pp. 272-273).

———— (1929). Feb. 19th letter to "A Country Lawyer." *Louis Marshall: Champion of Liberty,* ("Selected Papers and Addresses"), C. Reznikoff, ed., vol. II. Philadelphia: Jewish Publication Society of America (pp. 1145-1146).

_____ (1929). March 9th letter to Harold R. Medina. *Louis Marshall: Champion of Liberty* ("Selected Papers and Addresses"), C. Reznikoff, ed., vol. I. Philadelphia: The Jewish Publication Society of America (pp. 273-276).

Marshall, R. (ca. 1925). Unpublished letter from Robert Marshall to George Marshall, quoted in part by J.M. Glover (1986, pp. 79-81) in an unpublished manuscript, *Growth of a Forester*. Archived in the George Marshall papers at the Bancroft Library (collection #BANK MSS 79/95 carton 33) in folder 10 as "Writings Selected by George Marshall for a Book 1925-1962").

McCaughey, R.A. (2003). *Stand, Columbia; A History of Columbia University in the City of New York, 1754-2004.* New York: Columbia University Press.

Mendelson, A. (2008). *Exiles from Nowhere: The Jews and the Canadian Elite.* Montreal: Robin Brass Press Studio.

Miller, A.W. (1981). "The Founder of Ethical Culture." *Judaism,* vol. 30, pp. 377-380.

Morgenthau, H. (1922). *All in a Lifetime.* Garden City, N.Y.: Doubleday, Page & Co.

"N.Y. Alumni Association Meeting." *Cornell Daily Sun,* Apr. 20, 1885.

Ogden, R.M. (1959). "Preface." *The Diaries of Andrew D. White,* R.M. Ogden, ed. Ithaca, N.Y.: Cornell University Press (pp. v-vii).

Olan, L.A. (1951). *Felix Adler: Critic of Judaism and Founder of a Movement.* Gamoran, E., ed. New York: Union of American Hebrew Congregations.

"The Passport Question." *The American Jewish Year Book,* vol. 14, pp. 203-204.

Plunz, R. *et al.,* ed. (1999). *Two Adirondack Hamlets in History: Keene and Keene Valley.* Fleischmanns, N.Y.: Purple Mountain Press.

"Prof. Felix Adler's Betrothal." *New York Times,* Jan. 30, 1880.

Provol, W. L. (1937). *The Pack Pedder.* Chicago: John C. Winston Co.

Rayner-Canham, M. F. and G. W. (1992). "A Summer in the Adirondacks." *Harriet Brooks: Pioneer Nuclear Scientist.* Montreal: McGill-Queens University Press.

"A Report of Starvation and Destitution Among the Jews." *New York Times,* June 30, 1919.

Reznikoff, C., ed. (1957). *Louis Marshall: Champion of Liberty (Selected Papers and Addresses),* vol I & II. Philadelphia: Jewish Publication Society of America.

Ribak, G. (2014). "'The Jew Usually Left Those Crimes to Esau': The Jewish Responses to the Accusations about Criminality in New York, 1908-1913." *AJS Review,* vol. 38(1), pp. 1-28.

Rischin, M. (1962). *The Promised City: New York's Jews, 1897-1914.* Cambridge, Mass.: Harvard University Press.

Rock, H.B. (2012). "Upheaval, Innovation and Transformation: New York City Jews and the Civil War." *American Jewish Archives Journal,* vol. 64(1-2), pp. 1-26.

Rosenstock, M. (1965). *Louis Marshall: Defender of Jewish Rights.* Detroit: Wayne University Press.

Rosenzweig, S. (1992). *Freud, Jung, and Hall, the King-Maker: The Historic Expedition to America (1909) with G. Stanley Hall as Host and William James as Guest.* Kirkland, Wash.: Hogrefe & Huber (pp. 182-195).

Rudolph, B.G. (1970). *From a Minyan to a Community: A History of the Jews of Syracuse.* Syracuse, N.Y.: Syracuse University Press.

Sarna, J. (2020). "Interview." In *Moment* (summer issue, p. 69).

Schurman, J.G. (1892). "Inaugural Speech of Jacob Gould Schurman as 3rd Pres. of Cornell University."

"Sensation at Saratoga." *New York Times,* June 23, 1877.

Shevitz, A.H. (2007). *Jewish Communities on the Ohio River: A History.* Lexington, Ky.: University of Kentucky Press.

Silver, M.M. (2013). *Louis Marshall and the Rise of Jewish Ethnicity in America: A Biography.* Syracuse, N.Y.: Syracuse University Press.

Simon, L., ed. "An Adirondack Friendship" and "Josephine Clara Goldmark." In: *William James Remembered.* Lincoln, Neb.: University of Nebraska Press.

Stern, H. (2011). "Address of Dr. Horace Stern." *Memorial Addresses by Cyrus Adler, Irving Lehman, Horace Stern.* C. Adler & I. Lehman, eds. New York: The American Jewish Committee (pp. 106-115).

Stern, S.R., ed. (1876). *The Monthly Debater: Issued by Members of the Andrew Dickson White Debating Society* (pp. 24-32). World Jewish Congress Collection (#MS-361, Box 20, folder 3). Cincinnati: American Jewish Archives.

Straus, I. (1897). June 15th letter to Louis Marshall. *Louis Marshall and the Rise of Ethnicity in America: A Biography* by M.M. Silver (2013, pp. 11-12 & 547).

"Sunbeams." *Cornell Daily Sun,* Apr. 19, 1885.

Tatham, D. (2000). "Florine Stettheimer at Lake Placid, 1919: Modernism in the Adirondacks." *The American Art Journal,* vol. 31(1-2), pp. 4-31.

Taylor, C.M. (1892). Transcript of Nov. 11th prayer after "Inaugural Speech of Jacob Gould Schurman as 3rd President of Cornell University" (p. 81).

Thompson, N.L. (2001). "American Women Psychoanalysts 1911-1941." *The Annual of Psychoanalysis,* vol. 29: pp. 161-177.

"A Report of Starvation and Destitution Among the Jews." *New York Times,* June 30, 1919.

The Schwerner, Chaney, Goodman Memorial Project (2014). Cornell University Library Digital Collection (Campus Artifacts, Art & Memor-abilia Collection #511).

Urofsky, M.I. (2009). *Louis D. Brandeis: A Life.* New York: Pantheon Books.

Varoli, J. (2020). Oct. 26th column in *Russia Beyond the Headlines* titled "6 Great Americans Who Lived in Imperial Russia" (History Newsletter).

Villard, O.G. (1933). "Issues and Men." *The Nation,* vol. 137, no. 3564, pp. 473-474.

Weber, S. (2003). *The Finest Square Mile: Mount Jo and Heart Lake.* Fleischmanns, N.Y.: Purple Mountain Press.

Weingartner, F., ed. (1981). *Felix Adler and Ethical Culture: Memories and Studies.* New York: Columbia University Press.

Wessels, W. L. (1963). *Moses Cohen—Peddler to Capitalist: An Adirondack Pioneer Merchant.* Lake George, N.Y.: Adirondack Resorts Press, Inc.

Weston, H. (2008). *Freedom in the Wilds: An Artist in the Adirondacks,* 3rd ed. (Foster, R., editor and author of "Introduction"). Syracuse, N.Y.: University Press.

Whalen, M.L. (2003). "Gifts and Giving." *Cornell University Financial Plan, 2003-2005* (pp. 12-14).

Wheeler, J. (2019). "Shelley Orgel." *Graduate Society Bulletin of Psychoanalytic Association of New York,* vol. 57, p. 15.

Wisse, R.R. (2009). "The Shul at Loon Lake." *Commentary,* no. 128(3), pp. 38-42.

White, A.D. (1862). Sept.1st letter to Gerrit Smith catalogued as "Andrew D. White's Ideal University." Gerrit Smith Papers at Syracuse University Libraries Special Collections Research Center (Syracuse, N.Y.), library.syr.edu/digital/guides/s/smith_g.htm.

_____ (1873a). Apr. 9th holographic letter to unknown addressee [likely Joseph Seligman]. See MS #0011 of Felix Adler Papers at Butler Library of Columbia University (New York).

_____ (1873b). Dec. 19th transcript of testimony before the Senate of the State of New York (97th Session-1874). *Documents of the Senate of the State of New York,* vol. 6, p. 248. Albany, N.Y.: Weed, Parsons & Co. *Cf.* "A. D. White Papers" in the Cornell University Digital Repository (Ithaca, N.Y.).

_____ (1893). May 18th cable to U.S. State Department titled "Report of Minister White on Jewish Situation in Russia (St. Petersburg)." *White on Jewish Situation in Russia,* K. Stein, ed. (2010), https://israeled.org/resources/documents/white-on-jewish-situation-in-russia .

_____ (1905a). *Autobiography of Andrew D. White, Vol. I.* New York: The Century Co.

_____ (1905b). *Autobiography of Andrew D. White, Vol. II.* New York: The Century Co.

_____ (1906). June 5th letter to Francis Garrison in "A.D. White Papers" at Cornell University Digital Repository (Ithaca, N.Y.)

_____ (1911). "The Question Between the United States and Russia." Transcript of address given at a meeting under auspices of the National Citizens' Committee at Carnegie Hall on Dec. 6th (pp. 156-167). Catalogued at Cornell University Digital Repository (Ithaca, N.Y.), https://babel.hathitrust.org/cgi/pt?id=coo.3192410413208&view=2up&seq.=162.

_____ (1959). *The Diaries of Andrew D. White.* R.M. Ogden, ed. Ithaca, N.Y.: Cornell University Press.

About the Author

Lawrence M. Ginsburg, a native of upstate New York, now living in Georgia, is a retired lawyer with an interest in Jewish-American history. He is a graduate of Cornell University and the Syracuse University College of Law and a U.S. Army veteran. His previous publications include two monographs — *Israelites in Blue and Gray: Unchronicled Tales from Two Cities* (University Press of America, 2001) and *Tales of and About Jewish Youth During the Fin-de-siècle Era: An Annotated Gazette for a Transitional Decade in Upstate New York* (University Press of America, 2010) — and an essay, " 'Happyville' Deconstructed: An Over-caricatured Landmark in Southern Jewish History" (South Carolina Review, 2006). He has also authored or co-authored more than two dozen psychoanalytically oriented papers that have appeared in journals in North America, Europe and Israel.